WELLS: AN HISTORICAL GUIDE

Cover: View of Wells Cathedral by Jeremy Haslam

A glimpse through Penniless Porch into Market Place.

WELLS

An Historical Guide

Martin Langley
and
Edwina Small

Photographs by Peter Flatt

EX LIBRIS PRESS

First published in 1990 by
Ex Libris Press
1 The Shambles
Bradford on Avon
Wiltshire

Typeset in Plantin by Manuscript, Trowbridge
Printed by BPCC Wheatons Ltd., Exeter

© Martin Langley and Edwina Small

ISBN 0 848578 24 6

By the same authors and published by Ex Libris Press:
The Trams of Plymouth: a 73 Years Story (1990)

About the authors:

Martin Langley, one-time mariner and latterly English teacher in a Somerset comprehensive school, has since been writing books on nautical subjects. A local bookseller suggested the need for this book, and he accepted the challenge.

Edwina Small, co-author, is the Estimator's Assitant in the office of a well-known West Country builder's. Born and bred in the Wells district, she has gradually acquired an enviable collection of old postcard views of Wells and central Somerset.

CONTENTS

1	A Brief History	7
2	The Market Place	13
3	Wells Cathedral	21
4	The Bishop's Palace	35
5	The Liberty	41
6	High Street and Vicinity	51
7	Places of Worship	61
8	The Priory of St John and Almshouses	68
9	Schools and Hospitals	73
10	Round about Wells	81
11	Industrial Archaeology	87
12	Industry and Employment	94
	Notes	99
	Bibliography and Acknowledgements	103

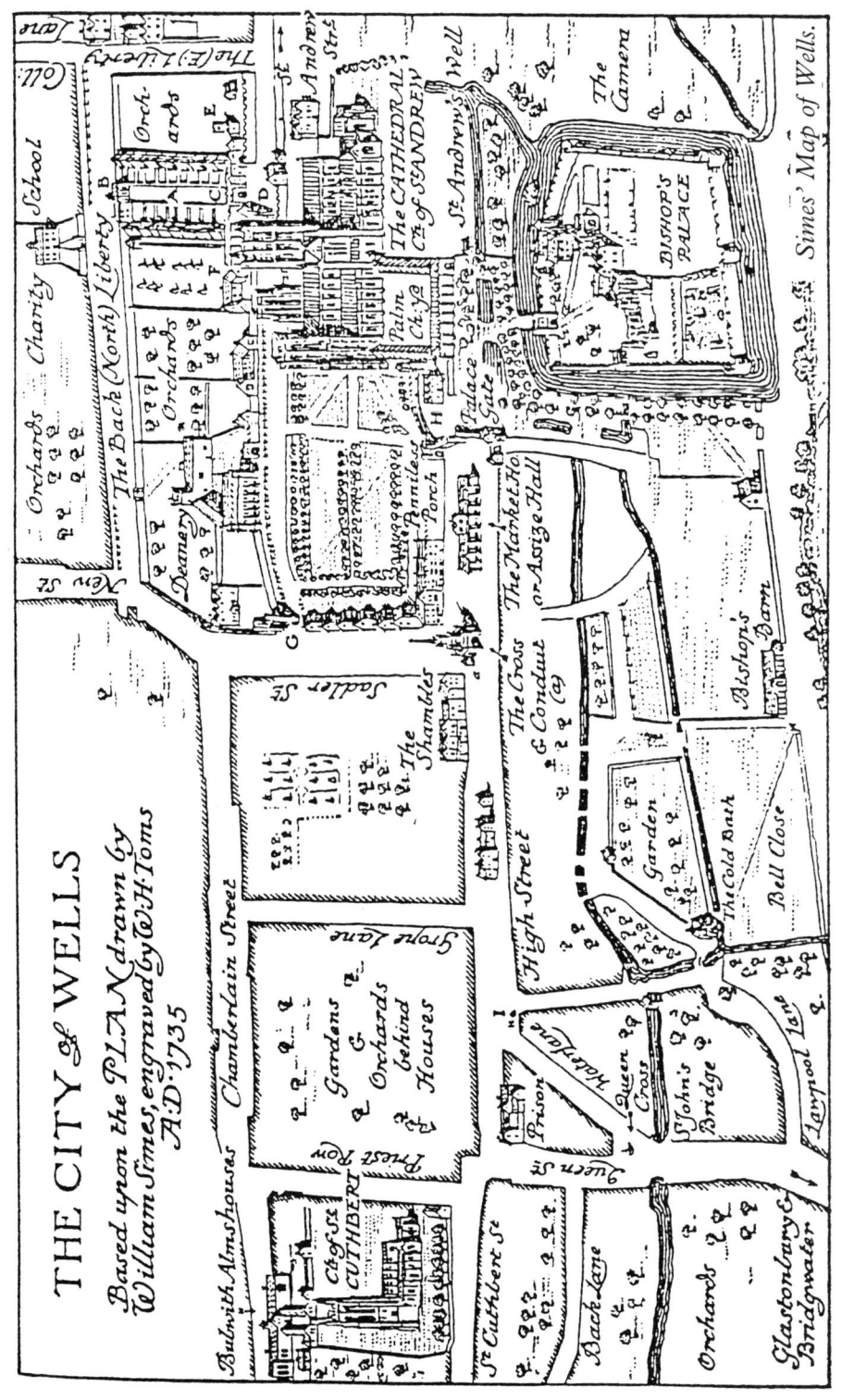

1 A BRIEF HISTORY

Somewhere in the mists of time Wells began life as a holy place. Ecclesiastical life came first, and civic life followed in its train. Wells, taking its name from the springs in the Bishop's palace grounds, was not a community which came to have a cathedral: it was a Cathedral which came to have a community. Tradition has always asserted that the first Church of St. Andrew was built near the wells in the year 705, founded by Ina, King of Wessex; and in recent years traces of its foundations have been discovered.

It was about two hundred years later that King Edward the Elder (son of Alfred the Great) chose Wells as the seat of the new bishopric of Somerset, appointed Aethelhelm as bishop in 909 and formed the new diocese known since the thirteenth century as Bath and Wells. About 1180 the building of the present cathedral began, to the north of the existing site of 705. A community was then gathering around the mother-church of the diocese to supply the varied needs of the ecclesiastical establishment; and the houses of the community formed the nucleus[1] of the future city of Wells.

The ecclesiastical population, comprising the Bishop's palace staff and estate workers, and the Dean and staff of the cathedral, soon came to number more than three hundred and some explanation of the latter is necessary here. In the Middle Ages, English cathedrals were either 'regular' or 'secular': that is to say, administered by monks under an abbot, as at Glastonbury and Bath, or by clergy under a dean, which was the case at Wells.

The form of administration had a considerable impact on the life of the lay community around. Whereas the abbeys had their monks in full-time residence and employment, were self-supporting, and often grew immensely rich, the canons of the cathedral, fifty in number, were only required to be in residence in Wells for one third of the year, and were free to take any clerical work elsewhere — *e.g.* as civil servants — for the other eight months. (*c.p.* the official designation of Church of England clergy today — 'clerk in holy orders'). The cathedral duties of the canons were performed vicariously in their absence by an equivalent number of minor canons or 'vicars'. These vicars have left their mark on the Wells of today, because the fourteenth century Vicars Close was built to house them, and the Chain Gate crossing St. Andrew's Street was erected in 1459 to give these 'vicars choral' access to and from the Cathedral without allowing exit to the town and its temptations.

The building of the Cathedral continued under successive bishops, the last construction being the fourteenth century retro-choir and lady chapel. The houses of the Cathedral dignitaries and some of the chapter canons, were mostly constructed during the fifteenth and sixteenth centuries in The Liberty, a large area of fifty-two acres to the north of the Cathedral, under the jurisdiction of the Dean and Chapter. The name Liberty denotes freedom or exemption from the taxes of the Bishop and the city, — an area with its own legislation. Starting in 1207 Bishop Jocelyn separated the Liberty from the rest of the city, and Bishop Burnell enclosed it with a battlemented wall in 1286. Penniless Porch in the Market Place and Brown's Gate in Sadler Street provided the access between the Liberty and the town.

Eleventh and Twelfth Centuries: The Domesday Survey of 1086 makes no mention of any township at Wells. No records bear testimony to civic life until 1136 when we hear of markets being held and the noise and disorder attendant on them incurring the bishop's displeasure.

Thirteenth Century: In 1201 Bishop Savaric gave the community a charter, which was ratified by King John, recognising Wells as a free borough and its people as free burghers. In effect this charter guaranteed the inhabitants their markets, fair days and security of land tenure. But it went no further, and in the centuries to come a state of tension existed between town and Bishop. It was undeniable that Wells owed its existence entirely to the Church, and undeniable that many of the Bishops had exercised a fostering care, and had been munificent in

A BRIEF HISTORY

improving the quality of life for their tenants. But as the town grew, the people yearned for complete independence of the Bishop's authority, and the bishops strove to maintain their overlordship.

Fourteenth Century: The town had been returning two members to Parliament from 1298, but these were chosen in the Hundred's Court under the Bishop's supervision. It was King Henry IV, at his accession in 1399, who granted Wells a charter which recognised the town as a corporate body, and this was confirmed by charters of Edward IV. Thereafter the members of Parliament were elected by the Burgesses and Freemen, with the mayor as the Returning Officer.

Fifteenth Century: Aside from the long drawn-out struggle for independence, civic life had been proceeding quietly without major event. The nearest Wells came to achieving notoriety was in 1471, when Margaret of Anjou, Queen of the deposed Henry VI, rode through Wells with her Lancastrian army to do battle with the Yorkist forces under Edward IV, in the Wars of the Roses. A few days' difference in the progress of their armies and Wells might have been the scene of Margaret's bloody defeat (three thousand dead), which took place at Tewkesbury on 10th May.

In 1497 Henry VII came to Wells with ten thousand cavalry on October 1st and lodged at the Deanery for one night. The King was displeased with the sympathy shown by the townspeople to Perkin Warbeck, pretender to the throne, and the town was fined £314.

Sixteenth Century: In 1539 Richard Whyting, the Lord Abbot of Glastonbury, was brought to Wells from the Tower of London for trial. He had refused to surrender his abbey to Thomas Cromwell's commissioners but the charge against him was that he had feloniously concealed from the King some of the abbey's valuables. Seated in a chair still preserved in the Bishop's Palace, he was arraigned in the Banqueting Hall on November 14th, and found guilty without, it appears, any trial at all. The next day he was hung, drawn and quartered on Glastonbury Tor.

The aspirations of the townsfolk for complete independence were realised after Bishop Thomas Godwin was appointed in 1584. He was sympathetic to the people's ambitions and paved the way for the

Charter of Queen Elizabeth Ist (July 1589) which declared that Wells should be 'a free city[2] and borough of itself'. Two courts were granted, and the right to operate a gaol, while the number of permitted annual fairs was increased from four to six.

Seventeenth Century: During the Civil War, 1642-5, Wells suffered considerably from the loutish behaviour of the soldiery on both sides. The city was occupied in turn by the Royalists (Sir Ralph Hopton) and Parliamentarians (Colonel Alexander Popham) in 1642, by the Royalists (Prince Maurice) again in 1643 and finally by the Parliamentarians (Lord Fairfax) in 1645. Roundhead troops plundered the cathedral, while damaging its statuary, and ransacked the Bishop's Palace: Cavaliers pillaged the town itself.

On 1st July 1685 Monmouth's army passed through Wells, five days before their defeat at Sedgemoor, the last battle on English soil. The disorderly troops stole the cathedral verge, wrecked the organ, damaged furniture, stabled horses in the nave and pulled statues from the west front. After Sedgemoor vengeance was swift. A commission headed by Lord Chief Justice Jeffreys arrived in the West Country. At Wells, one of the six centres where Jeffreys sat in judgement, the prisoners were tried, sentenced and executed with indecent haste. On the last day of the Assize, 23rd September 1685, 543 were condemned of whom 383 were sentenced to transportation. A few escaped while being marched from Wells. Nine were hanged at Wells[3], in a field still known as Gallows Close, beyond Keward Bridge.

William Penn the Quaker came to Wells in 1695 and obtained permission to preach in the Market House. This permission was then withdrawn, but Penn addressed a crowd said to number about 2,500 from a bay window on the first floor of the Crown Inn. He was then arrested and gaoled by the Mayor but the Bishop intervened to give him a licence and secure his release.

Eighteenth Century: The city treasury financed the erection of a 50-faggot bonfire in 1704, lit to celebrate Marlborough's victory at Blenheim on 13th August.

The Assizes were held in the city for the first time on August 11th 1727, and a house in New Street was later acquired for the Judge's Lodging. Wells remained an assize town for the following fifty years.

A BRIEF HISTORY

Susannah Bruford, a local housewife, was burned at the stake at Cure Green, Wells in 1753, for the murder of her husband.

In 1754 the Corporation, worried by a considerable increase in the number of beggars, especially females, who were pestering the community, appointed a beadle to whip the beggars and physically drive them out of town. Harsh measures indeed!

Nineteenth Century: In the mid-nineteenth century three railways reached Wells and built stations — which were not linked by rail! — within a third of a mile of each other! The Somerset Central line (later the Somerset & Dorset) to Glastonbury was opened amid great public rejoicing on 3rd March, 1859. The East Somerset Railway to Witham opened on 1st March, 1862. The Bristol & Exeter line to Yatton was ready on 5th April, 1870. These two latter railways were absorbed by the GWR in 1876. Rail connections and through running began in 1879.

Twentieth Century: In the Great War of 1914-18 Wells, which had then a population of 4,600, lost 99 men on active service in the armed services. They are commemorated on the memorial erected in St. Cuthbert churchyard.

In World War II, with a population of 4,800, Wells casualty list of serving men was 38. The city took in many evacuee children and there was a prisoner-of-war camp at Penleigh, which is now the site of the electronics firm EMI, Wells's largest employer.

Mary Bignal Rand, born in Tucker Street, Wells and educated at Kennion Road School, brought honour to the city when she won a gold medal at the Tokyo Olympics in 1964 with a winning long jump of 22 feet 2 inches. Wells Town Clerk Harold Dodd responded to the news immediately with a congratulatory wire in Mary's home dialect: "Us be turrable proud of 'ee". This jump is commemorated by a pavement brass on the north side of the market place.

2 THE MARKET PLACE

Whether it be a tour on foot, or an armchair study of Wells, there is probably no better place to start than where we left the last chapter's history — at the Mary Bignal Rand pavement brass in the **Market Place**. Here the historical three spheres of influence met. Penniless Porch leads directly into the Liberty, the domain of the Dean & Chapter; the splendid gate known as the Bishop's Eye gives access to the Palace and what was once the bishop's vast estate; while around is the Market Place, the heart-beat of civic life, scene of fairs and markets, the province of the Mayor and Corporation.

The **Bishop's Eye** gate dominates the Market Place. Including a house on either side, it was built by Bishop Bekynton in the mid-fifteenth century, where before there had been only a high wall with a small arch. Dormer windows in the northernmost house and a ground floor front extension to the other detracted from the original symmetry in the eighteenth century, but today the Bishop's Eye remains the kingpin of the Market Place and the most imposing of Wells's several medieval gateways.

Penniless Porch was also built by Bishop Bekynton and his arms are sculpted on the north side. The gate was so named because it became a resort of beggars waylaying pilgrims for money, passing to and from the Cathedral.

Adjoining Penniless Porch on the north side is a fine row of twelve houses which originally backed on to the wall of the Liberty and were known as the 'New Work'; but have long been in use as shops or offices. Again, Bishop Bekynton was responsible, and he would have matched them with a similar row on the south side had not his death intervened.

Opposite: Reconstruction of The High Cross as it would have appeared, according to the available evidence (specially drawn by H.J.A. Strik)

WELLS: AN HISTORICAL GUIDE

*Wells Market Place: the gateways —
Bishop's Eye (right); Penniless Porch (left).*

Leland, Henry VIII's much-travelled antiquary, was most impressed with the 'New Work', describing them as 'right exceeding Fair Houses al uniforme of Stone high and fair windoid'.

Two hundred years later a less pretentious row of houses was built behind them, facing the Cathedral Green; and most of the curtain wall has disappeared since the two rows were gradually united to create larger premises. Bekynton's houses stopped short of the corner, where the Midland Bank now stands. This is on the site of two houses which were in occupation when the New Work began building. A large general store, Holloway & Clare, occupied the eastern half of the New Work buildings in the first quarter of this century.

Although the north and east sides of the Market Place are in essence little altered from Bekynton's day, the remainder has seen considerable change. Where the present **Conduit** with its Rotary wishing well stands today, Bekynton had built a large, four-square conduit designed

The Conduit, built 1796, in Market Place.

15

to harmonize with the nearby High Cross. Conduit wardens were appointed from 1513 to regulate the flow of water. Bekynton's conduit was surmounted by the Market Bell, and a Corporation Order of July 2nd forbad any trading before the bell had sounded permission. In 1756 the structure was pulled down because of dilapidation. The present conduit, by Masters, a builder of Bath, was erected for a cost of £150 to replace it.

The **High Cross of Wells**, where the Bishop's bailiff read out notices and proclamations, is depicted on Simes' 1755 map of Wells. It is known that the Cross was there when Bishop Bekynton built his conduit, but it is not clear whether it stood to the east or west of the conduit. Sherwin Bailey notes that fifteenth century records describe the first house on the north side of Market Place (site of present Midland Bank) as 'opposite the High Cross of Wells'. If this was so, the Cross would seem to have been west of the conduit, at the junction with Sadler Street. Simes' map shows both cross and conduit in the middle of the road corner, with the cross to the east. Serel says it stood east of the conduit and that its removal about 1780 was due to weakening caused by demolition of the adjacent Exchequer in the middle of the square. Part of the cross fell, says Holmes, and the Bishop gave permission for it to be dismantled and the material safely stored, presumably with a view to possible re-erection. Restoration does not seem to have been considered however and the fate of the stored stonework is unknown.

The **Exchequer** in the Market Place, built in 1542 by Dean Woolman and Bishop Knight, was one of several public rooms in ancient Wells. (The others were the Linen Hall over the High Street Shambles, the Guild Hall at the 1436 Bubwith Almshouses, the Burgesses' Room at the City gate, and possibly a Bishop's hall of which the site is not known). Described by a contemporary writer as 'a right sumptuous piece of work', the Exchequer[4] seems to have served as the Town Hall, and was built on pillars over the site of what was formerly a stagnant pool in the market place. The open ground floor, which provided a roof for stalls on market days, was probably damp and draughty. Nevertheless it was used by the Assizes and Sessions, when it was screened and curtained.

The building was repaired in 1663 and 1687 and the city fire engine was stabled in the undercroft from 1702. The upper floor was divided

THE MARKET PLACE

into two rooms — the council chamber and a wool store. A cornice bore the date 1542 and a Latin inscription, and at the west end was a Horologe — the public clock, maintained by the Corporation. After the functions of the Exchequer had passed to the Town Hall, Law Courts, and Market House, it was pulled down in the mid-nineteenth century, apparently at the request of a disgruntled tradesman who protested that it was an impediment to his view and to his business.

The present **Town Hall**, **Lawcourts** and **Gaol** were erected in 1779 on the site of a canonical house, which had once served as the Archdeacon's official residence. The purchase of this house and erection of the new buildings were authorised by an Act of Parliament during the reign of George III. Behind the site of the old canonical house had run the south-easterly access in and out of Wells — the road to Shepton Mallet, roughly following the course of the present footpath to Dulcote. Bishop Jocelyn obtained a licence from King John to divert this road, in 1207, making his palace more secluded, and to enclose the woods where are now the Park meadows, making his estate more extensive. Ever since, it has been necessary to make a considerable detour, via the Liberty and Tor Street, when travelling between Wells and Shepton Mallet. Many visitors must wonder why there is no south-easterly road from the Market Place; but there was, — nearly eight hundred years ago!

The present **Post and Sorting Office**, between the Bishop's Eye and the Town Hall, was originally built in 1836 as a colonnaded Market House to replace the facilities formerly afforded by the Exchequer Undercroft. Conversion to local Head Post Office came about in 1923, and was achieved, as is still evident, by building windowed walls between the pillars. The adjacent mail van garage is also a conversion. This building formerly housed the Corporation committees' room at the north end, its walls lined with portraits of past mayors; while the south end formed the City Fire Station prior to its removal to Prince's Road in 1937. Before the introduction of motor fire engines, Wells firemen answering a call had first to run to Park Woods where the horses were grazed!

The most prominent building on the south side of Market Place is the fifteenth century Crown Inn, where the Quaker William Penn preached and was arrested, in 1695. The Crown resulted from the uniting of three terraced houses, dating from *c.* 1450, and successive

The fifteenth century Crown Hotel.

THE MARKET PLACE

owners have preserved the authenticity of the interior. For a while, during the nineteenth century the inn was disused and derelict, but more prosperous days returned and the Crown absorbed its eastern neighbour, the Royal Oak, now re-titled the Penn Eating Room.

Adjacent on the west side is the **Red Lion**, dating from about 1600. Never a staging post, because during the coaching era it was a temperance house. A stone fireplace and an upper stairway, both seventeenth century, have been preserved and are worthy of notice.

The shop premises immediately west of the Red Lion bear a brass plaque commemorating the gift to the townspeople by Bishop Richard in 1803 of water from his wells 'For the purpose of cleansing the town, and if occasion should require it, of extinguishing fires'. This is the water that flows daily along the wide gutters of High Street, Broad Street and St. Cuthbert Street.

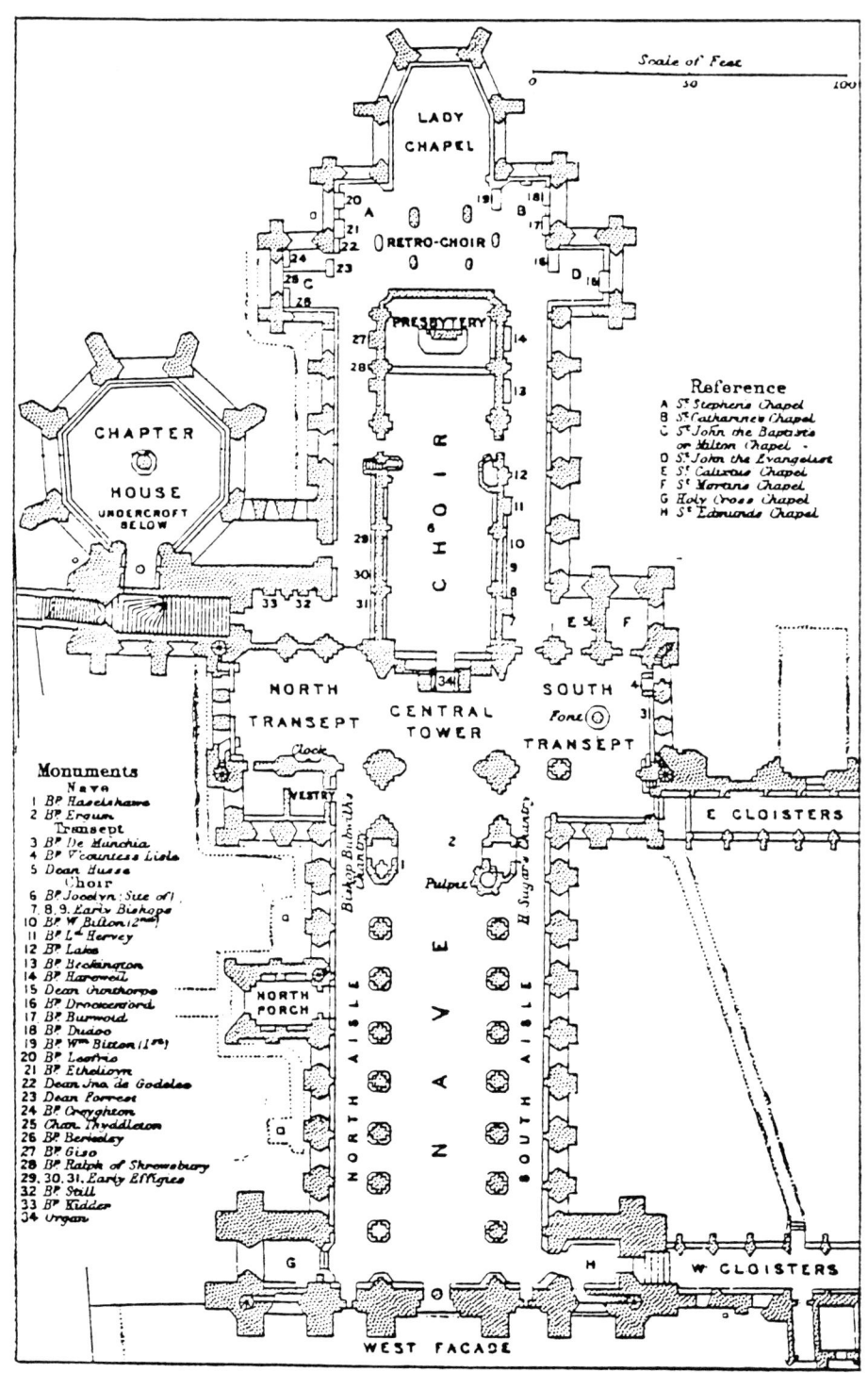

Plan of Wells Cathedral (by kind permission of Ward Lock Ltd.)

3 WELLS CATHEDRAL

Wells is not one of the largest English cathedrals, but it is certainly one of the most impressive. It is in a beautiful setting, a backdrop of old-world dwellings and gardens; has a magnificent statue-bedecked west front of world-wide renown; and its interior, uncluttered by the mural tablets — most were transferred to the cloisters in the 1820s — is dominated by the great fourteenth century engineering feat of the reversed arches. Moreover Wells has survived eight centuries with all its associated buildings around it — the magnificent chapter house, the cloisters, the Bishop's Palace, the deanery, various prebendal houses and the unique Vicars' Close — all treasures from the thirteenth to fifteenth centuries.

The original church on the site is believed to have been built by King Ina of the West Saxons between 695 and 707AD, beside the springs which were possibly regarded as a holy well, and dedicated to St. Andrew. St. Andrew's Church became a cathedral in 909AD when the first Bishop of Wells, Athelm, was appointed by King Edward the Elder, and the see was formed. The bones of seven Saxon bishops buried in the original church were transferred when it was dismantled in 1195, and their tombs can be seen in the quire aisles. The ancient hexagonal font in the south transept today is very probably from the old cathedral, as may also be much of the stone work of the north porch. The foundations of this earlier church have been revealed by archaeological excavations in recent years between the cloisters and the wells. Its chapel of St. Mary was retained and restored as a Lady Chapel to the present cathedral, 1196 - *c*. 1450.

In or about 1180 Bishop Reginald began building the present cathedral, and the work proceeded for nearly sixty years, using stone from Doulting quarries, eight miles distant. From 1206 the work was

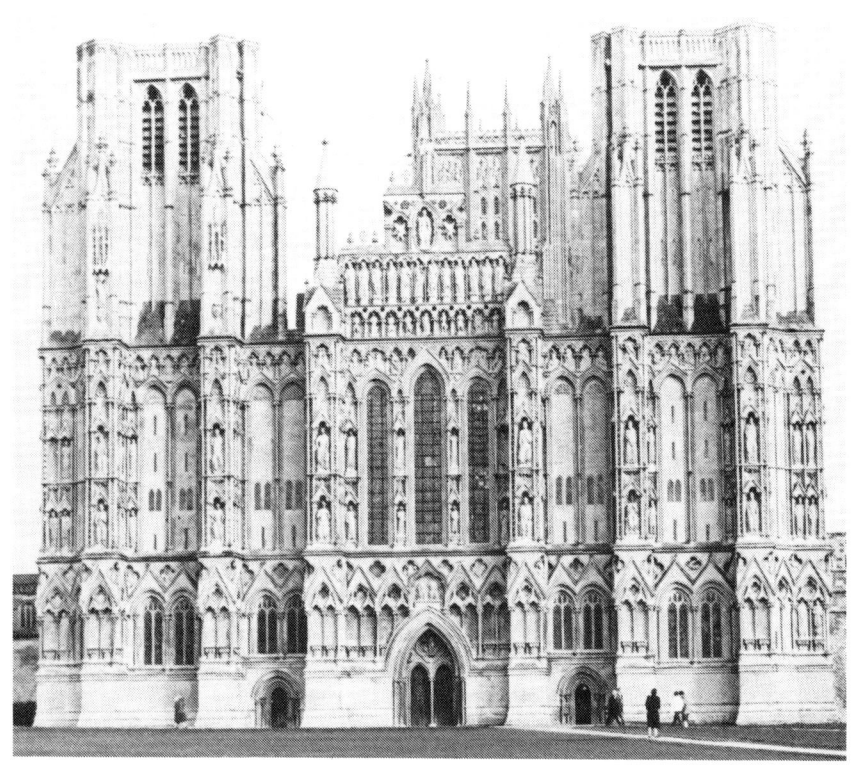

Cathedral, West Front — as built, there were 366 figures.

THE CATHEDRAL

inspired by Bishop Jocelyn, whose brother Hugh, Bishop of Lincoln, subscribed lavishly toward it. In 1239 the still incomplete building was consecrated, by which time the nave and transepts were finished and work on the central tower and west front had begun. The work was brought to a halt between 1208 and 1213, when the Pope placed England under an Interdict because of a dispute with King John. Jocelyn was among bishops who had to flee the country to escape the King's fury; all churches were closed, and services forbidden. Between 1290 and 1340 the central tower, new east end with lady chapel and the chapter house were completed. The west towers and cloisters followed, and some alterations to the quire, c. 1345-50. The cathedral was thus in building over a period of more than one hundred and fifty years.

The exterior feature for which Wells is everywhere known is the **West Front**, an immense masonry screen whose design is carried across the flanking towers and which originally carried 366 sculpted figures. Its significance in architecture is that it is the forerunner of the great Gothic façades of European cathedrals, the earliest of which are later by more than half a century. Built by Bishop Jocelyn, between 1220 and 1240, in pure Early English style, Wells has a unique place as the oldest work of its kind in Christendom — a lone precursor of things to come. Criticism is sometimes made that the West Front lacks the height to match its width, and that the western doorways are too small in proportion to the whole, but what is not questionable is that the statuary which the front was designed to display is of the highest artistic merit. Looking up at the great façade from the Cathedral Green, it is apparent that the statuary is arranged in three stages:–

1. The crowning gable or central pediment — 3 tiers, 24 figures.
2. The superstructure — 3 tiers, 205 figures.
3. The base — a single tier of twin niches which held slightly oversize figures, with small sculpted groups in recesses, 137 figures.

The Central Pediment top tier had Christ Enthroned in Glory as the centrepiece, with the Virgin Mary and John the Baptist on either side. Sadly, Monmouth's uncouth troops in 1685, who had gained the cathedral roof to steal lead for bullets, destroyed these three statues. The two side figures were crowbarred out and sent crashing; the less accessible figure of Christ was battered out of recognition and shot at by musketeers below. In 1986 these three statues were replaced by a new sculpture of Christ in Majesty, while emblematic figures of the

WELLS: AN HISTORICAL GUIDE

New amongst old — David Wynne's 'Christ in Majesty' crowning the medieval statues.

six–winged seraphim were substituted in the side niches. The sculptor was David Wynne.

The middle tier of the pediment displays figures of the twelve apostles, and the bottom row the Nine Orders of Angels.

The super-structure statuary begins with the cornice, which is a tier of small canopied niches holding an unusual series of eighty-five sets of nude figures representing the Rising from the Dead on the Last Day. The other two tiers comprise a galaxy of 120 larger figures of Saints, Martyrs, Kings, Queens, Bishops and Monks — each a historical character, but no longer identifiable. About ten figures are missing, due to the depradations of Protestant barbarians of the sixteenth and seventeenth centuries.

The Base has suffered most, from the mindless excesses of anti-Prayer Book protestors in 1549, Cromwell's Roundheads in the Civil War, and Monmouth's levies in 1685. Most of the sixty-two large statues are missing but they are considered to have been saints and prophets. The quatre-foils, containing seventy-five figures in Biblical

THE CATHEDRAL

episodes (New Testament, northside; Old Testament, southside) and Angels rising from clouds, have likewise suffered many losses and much damage.

The twin **Western Towers** are 150 feet in height, the design of William Wynford, and their flat tops lead many to suppose that they are incomplete. In fact their truncated appearance is designed to give pre-eminence to the central tower. The twin towers are not identical. The north-west tower was built around 1325-35 by Bishop Stafford, with money bequeathed by his predecessor Bishop Bubwith. It has canopied niches (which the other tower has not) and the northern niche holds a (1980) statue of Bubwith in prayer. The south-west tower was built about fifty years earlier by Bishop Harewell, and contains the heaviest ring of ten bells in the world. The tenor weighs 56 cwt.

The **Central Tower** (164 feet), massive and pinnacled, is not the original. Its smaller predecessor was completed by Bishop Reginald in the early thirteenth century, and was partly demolished by an earthquake in 1248. Its rebuilding, begun by Bishop Bytton in 1263, was completed by Bishop Drokensford in 1322. But it had now been carried to a greater height than the original and the piers began to show signs of collapse under the extra weight. In 1338 the remedy of the inverted arches[5] was applied to avert the fall of the tower. Erected on three sides only, they have since been a principal feature of the interior.

Inside, the **Nave** has nine bays to the crossing of the transepts, the Gothic arches, which have been described as 'pointed Romanesque', being supported by massive grouped piers. The beautiful and varied capitals of these piers deserve special notice. One by the north porch depicts an animal licking his fur and birds preening their feathers; also a lively figure of a ram and a staff-carrying bird with a human head. The second pier beyond has a representation of an angry man with a club chasing a fox which is making off with his goose. There are equally fascinating capitals on the south side. The Triforium (the arcading between the main arches and the clerestory) boasts a Minstrel's Gallery above the sixth arch on the south side.

Although the nave appears a homogenous whole, sharper eyes will detect where the construction was interrupted during the reign of King John. The point of meeting is between the fifth and sixth bays from the west where a difference is apparent in the hood moulds (highest rib of the arches) and the sculptured heads at the meeting of the mould

The inverted arches of 1388.

Sculptured capitals — plucking a thorn.

arching are not continued; while larger stones have been used in the later, western work. In the ninth bay of the nave are two chantry chapels, constructed between the piers. Chantry chapels were endowed for saying mass daily for the soul of the founder. On the north side is the Bubwith chantry, of 1429, commemorating the Bishop who endowed the north-west tower and gave the city an almshouse: on the south side the Sugar chantry of 1489 — Sugar was a fifteenth century canon Treasurer. Placed centrally in the floor at the head of the nave is a stone bearing witness to the cathedral's founder with the simple inscription; INA REX 688-726. (The dates are those of his amazing thirty-eight years of Kingship).

The **Transepts**, although built before the nave, have capitals and corbels of a later period, which suggests restoration work after damage when the tower fell in the earthquake of 1248. The capitals in the transepts are particularly interesting and with those in the nave constitute a unique treasure of Wells — nothing quite like them can be found anywhere else. The many topics they depict include scenes from peasant life of the thirteenth century, including The Apple Stealers, a strip cartoon in sculpture; and the 'toothache capitals'. These latter are due to the reverence given to Bishop William Bytton II (1266-74), who had remarkably fine and healthy teeth into old age in times when this was a rarity — which the locals attributed to his saintly life. A visit to his shrine was considered a cure for dental troubles.

The north transept had two chapels on its eastern side, but entrance is via the quire aisle. The outer was the Chapel of the Holy Cross, containing the tomb of Bishop Kidder (1691-1703) who with his wife was killed in the palace by the fall of a chimney-stack during the hurricane which swept the south-west on 26th November, 1703. Beside the tomb is a figure of Kidder's daughter looking with distress on the funeral urns of her parents. The former chapel of St. David, in the inside position, contains the tomb of Bishop Still (1593-1607) with his effigy in episcopal robes. Also in the north transept is the famous clock, constructed, according to a cherished but unsubstantiated tradition, about 1390 by Peter Lightfoot, a monk of Glastonbury, who had made a very similar clock for the abbey. This clock and its automatic moving figures are the popular showpiece of Wells and have drawn the crowds since tourism began. It is a misconception that the clock formed part of the spoils of Glastonbury Abbey, for it was here

The clock (outside) — the quarter jacks (Knights with halberds).

two hundred years before the suppression of the monastery. This is the second oldest clock in existence; Salisbury's — which has no dial — being a few years earlier.

The north transept also gives access to a stone staircase which has no equal in English cathedrals. After eighteen steps the stairway divides so that one part goes forward to the Chain-Gate Bridge while the other swerves to the **Chapter House**. Built between 1290 and 1302, the Chapter House (where the canons met daily for Bible reading and frequently for Cathedral business) is an octagonal hall in the Decorated style, with a vaulted ceiling and a four-light window on each side. Both from within and without, it is a very beautiful building, but its position here, instead of off the cloisters, is unusual. The south transept, like the north, also has two chapels on its eastern side, dedicated to St. Calixtus (next the quire aisle) and St. Martin. The latter has been made into a war memorial.

Also in the south transept is the **Font**, the oldest relic in the Cathedral and probably transferred from the earlier building. A narrow door in the south-east corner once gave access to the old Lady Chapel in the cloister.

The **Quire** consists of six bays, — the western three, up to the pulpit, being the original east end of Bishop Reginald's building; the eastern three the work of Bishops Drokensford and Ralph, about one hundred and fifty years later. The Bishop's throne (cathedra, hence the cathedral) is in the Perpendicular style and thought to date from around 1350, though much altered by restorations. The Prebendal Stalls, backed by panels of colourful embroidery made 1935-45 and the stalls for the choir, replaced the originals in 1848.

High on the east wall and above the retro-quire is the great medieval **Jesse Window** — its theme the descent of Jesus Christ from Jesse, father of King David. The tendrils of a vine curl around the kings and prophets descended from him and the glass is rich in colour.

The north quire aisle gives access to the **Undercroft**, which is the basement, on ground level, of the chapter house. By the inside entrance door, which has elaborate wrought-iron hinges, is an unusual stone lantern. In the south quire aisle is the tomb of Bishop Bytton II and it can be seen that some of the toothache-sufferers who have pilgrimaged here have chipped away fragments of stone to take back with them. In 1848 the coffin was opened, in the presence of the Dean, and the

The Cathedral from the north-east.

Steps from the Cathedral to the Chain Gate (ahead) and the Chapter House (right). This must be the finest stone stairway in the West Country.

Bishop's skeleton was found to have an absolutely perfect set of teeth, undecayed and scarcely discoloured.

The **Retro-Quire** — the processional space between the Quire and the Lady Chapel — is by virtue of its slender, graceful vaulting, one of the special beauties of Wells cathedral. Here may be seen a thirteenth century semi-circular cope chest, still used for its original purpose of stowing vestments with a single fold. On either side the chapels of St. John the Baptist and St. John the Evangelist respectively form small transepts.

The **Lady Chapel**, eastern termination of the four hundred feet long cathedral, is a five-sided apse, its five great windows filled with fragmented medieval glass which has been replaced more or less at random after destruction of the originals by the iconoclasts of past ages.

To the south of the Cathedral is the **Cloister**, of which the east side, with the cathedral library above, was built by Bishop Bubwith's executors, about 1427; and the west side, with choir school and singing room above, by Bishop Bekynton in 1457. Immediately west of the cloister, Bekynton also built a house for the organist and master of the choristers. It was damaged by fire about 1550, part was demolished in 1869, and the roof of the remainder fell in as a result, in 1870. The gable end of this **Quirister's House** remains today, amid a pleasant garden dedicated to the memory of Mary Mitchell, wife of Patrick Mitchell, Dean of Wells, 1973-89.

The West cloister singing room and the garden of the Quirister's House were occupied by the Wells High School for Girls[6] from 1888-1965.

To those interested in architecture, historic buildings or sculptured art, Wells Cathedral will richly repay several visits and the study of books providing much more information than is given here.

Finally, beyond any doubt the Cathedral Choir (sixteen boys, eleven men) is one of the glories of Wells. No visitors with the time to attend a service at which they are singing should allow the opportunity to pass them by.

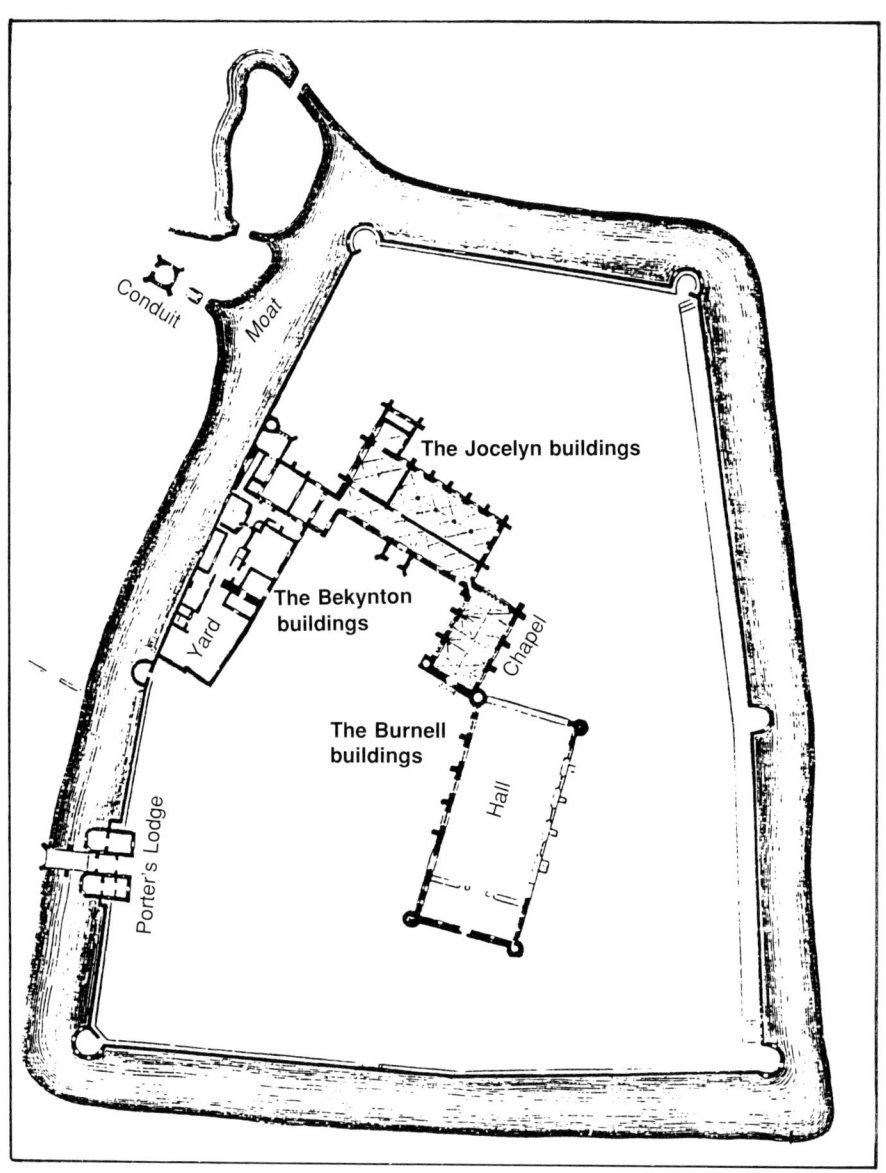

4 THE BISHOP'S PALACE

Wells is a city of superlatives, and there can surely be no other episcopal residence nor stately home in the realm to excel in loveliness the palace of the Bishops of Bath & Wells. Among the seventy-four prelates who have held the see were two famous absentee landlords: Thomas Wolsey (1518-23), the catalyst of the Reformation, and William Laud (1626-28), later Charles I's ill-fated Archbishop of Canterbury. They were reputed not once to have visited their palace at Wells, so can never have been aware of what they were missing. Today the seven hundred year-old palace still stands serene behind its moat and battlemented curtain wall, still preserving its thirteenth, fourteenth and fifteenth century buildings only superficially altered.

In the time of the first Bishop of Wells, Athelm (900-23), there was quite certainly a group of clergy who were housed together with him. Nothing is known of their number nor of their communal dwelling. However, it is known that Bishop Giso (1061-88) provided accomodation for his canons which included a refectory and a dormitory. It is likely that he had his own quarters in the same building. He also placed his priests under the Rule of St. Chrodegang[7] which gave them an ordered life, yet without making them monks. His successor Bishop John (1088-1123), had other ambitions. He obtained from William Rufus and the Pope the abbey and the city of Bath, and transferred there the headquarters and title of the diocese, and his permanent residence. He pulled down Giso's house, turned out the canons to fend for themselves, and built at Wells a secondary manor for himself, probably on the site of the present palace. There followed a period of more than

---

Opposite: Plan of the Bishop's Palace (reproduced with acknowledgement from J.H.Parker's The Architectural Antiquities of Wells).

a century when the Bishops lived at Bath or Glastonbury[8], and the bishop's residence at Wells remained no more than a secondary manor.

It was Bishop Jocelyn (1206-44), a native of Wells, who made the city of his birth again the centre of the diocese, and began building the palace we see today. Moreover, he obtained from King John permission to create a park in the meadows and woods to the south. Today, what remains of this estate is in the possession of the Church Commissioners and includes the Dulcote footpath where Wells dogowners are wont to exercise their pets, and the trackbed of the former GWR line to Witham.

On days when the palace is open to the public, admittance is given to the **Jocelyn buildings**, which form the central portion of the present palace. Jocelyn built the ground floor chambers today known as the Undercroft; the Entrance Hall with a gallery above and spiral staircases in south-west and north-west turrets: a Great Hall, then open up to the roof but now ceilinged and sectioned into Drawing Room and Library.

The one-time living quarters over the Entrance Hall are now the **Long Gallery**. Here can be seen the Coronation Cope[9] worn by Bishops of Bath & Wells since 1902; a fifteenth century chair used, according to tradition, by Abbot Whyting of Glastonbury at his trial; and the original Glastonbury Chair, from which all others of the design have been copied. The **Conference Room** (originally part of the Hall) and the **Panelled Room** (originally Jocelyn's solar), are both accessible to the public and contain portraits of former Bishops of Bath and Wells. The Jocelyn building is now known as the Henderson Rooms, Bishop Henderson (1960-75) having restored them to their present condition and use.

In about 1290 Bishop Burnell (1275-92) built the great **Banqueting Hall** and then the Chapel. The Chapel bridged the gap between the new hall and the Jocelyn buildings. A peculiarity is that the northeast turret of the hall serves also as a south-west turret to the Chapel. It has a window which would have been useless had the chapel been already there. The Banqueting Hall was 115 feet long by 60 feet wide and had a large porch on the north side. There was a kitchen, pantry and buttery, and over them a solarium for the bishop's private use. It was a hall befitting the entertainment of Kings and great men.

Here Edward III spent the Christmas of 1331, presumably with his queen Philippa and the infant Black Prince. In this hall Abbot Whyting

THE BISHOP'S PALACE

Burnell's great Banquetting Hall.

of Glastonbury was sentenced to death for refusing to surrender the abbey to Cromwell's parliament. From here he was taken to be hung on Glastonbury Tor. The hall stood for 260 years. Bishop Barlow (1548-54) then decided he had no use for it and obtained Crown permission to sell it to Sir John Gates, King's Commissioner, who stripped the roof and windows and sold the timber, lead and glass, but left the four walls standing. (Gates had already done the same with the chancel of Pleshey Church in Essex. It is scarcely sad therefore to record that he was executed by Mary I for treason, in 1553). Two hundred and eighty years later, Bishop Law (1824-43) demolished the east and south walls, leaving the south-east turret standing solitarily, merely to increase the lawn area. For their acts of vandalism in wrecking one of the loveliest edifices in Wells no excuse can be found for either Bishop Barlow or Bishop Law. It was wanton destruction. Today the north and west walls and the lone turret still stand, ruinous but magnificent. The **Chapel**, in the Decorated style, is dedicated to the Holy Trinity. It was largely refurnished in the nineteenth century by volunteer craftsmen from Somerset parishes.

Bishop Ralph (1329-63) constructed the moat — by a diversion of St. Andrew's stream from the wells — and erected the curtain wall with its gateway and bastion towers, following a licence to crenellate granted by the Crown in 1340. The townspeople had been in dispute with the Bishop, wishing to gain independence and freedom from dues. A charter they obtained to this effect was overturned by the courts when the Bishop appealed to the Crown and was able to show that the townspeople were his tenants. But bad feeling was aroused between Bishop and people, and the fortification of the palace was the result.

The **Gatehouse drawbridge** was in working order as late as the 1930's, when it was converted to a roadway. It was last raised in 1831 when the Bristol Riots over the Reform Bill caused anxiety. But the palace fortifications have never been put to the test of attack and defence, though Cromwell's soldiers rushed in virtually unopposed in 1642 and ransacked the interior. Below a window on the east side of the Gatehouse is a bell which the swans on **the moat** are trained to ring when they want food. This practice has become widely known and in Wells Museum can be seen, embalmed, the first swan taught to use the bell, by the daughter of Bishop Hervey (1969-94).

The raised walk along the bank of the moat at the foot of the walls was a favourite haunt of Bishop Ken (1685-91) who is said to have composed his popular morning and evening hymns 'Awake, my soul' and 'Glory to Thee my God' while meditating here, a felicitous if unconfirmed legend.

Every summer the moat is encumbered by blanketweed and duckweed. At season's end the duckweed dies away but the blanketweed requires stronger measures, and a weed-boat is hired for a week from the British Waterways Board to deal with it. This is a steel paddle-wheel craft powered by diesel-hydraulics, which first cuts the weed from the bottom and then scoops it from the surface. This interesting craft comes by road from South Wales and is hoisted in and out of the moat by the crane of its own lorry.

The north-west bastion Tower, opposite which summer visitors are wont to feed the ducks and geese, was originally used as a prison for 'criminous clerks' (law breaking clergy) and had a guardhouse on the upper floor. Under the north-east bastion is an eight feet high sculpture in yew of Adam and Eve, the work of E.J.Clack in 1948. Bishop Henderson (1960-75) instituted an annual boat race on the moat as

The Bishop's Palace — sixteenth century gatehouse and drawbridge

part of a fete in the palace grounds to benefit local charities.

The last substantial addition to the palace was the **northern block**, erected by Bishop Bekynton (1443-65), consisting of hall, kitchen, parlour, gate, tower — and a cloister later demolished. Bishop Clerk (1533-41) enlarged and improved this building, and put in two oriel windows overlooking the moat. The interior was modernised by Bishop Bradfield (1946-60) and forms the living-quarters of the bishop today.

Within the grounds lie the **wells** which give the city its name. Possibly misled by the city's coat of arms, depicting three traditional brick-walled wells, visitors are sometimes suprised to find a kidney-shaped pond. It was dug at an unknown date to enclose the springs which have bubbled up from time immemorial, and to contain the water from creating a marsh. This pool is where all things began for Wells. It is the city's *raison d'etre*.

Swans on the moat, 1990.

5 THE LIBERTY

The Liberty is an area of more than fifty acres on the north side of the Cathedral, which was made separate from the rest of the city by Bishop Jocelyn in 1207, and free from civic jurisdiction until the last century. English cathedrals typically have a close or precinct adjacent, with some prebendal houses: but Wells is unique in having this large designated area containing the old Deanery and most of the original — if much rebuilt — canonical houses still standing and for the most part still devoted to ecclesiastical use. In 1285-6 Bishop Burnell enclosed the Liberty with a battlemented wall, of which traces can still be found behind the houses on the north side of Market Place and the east side of Sadler Street. The two sides of the wall were indeed different worlds. The Liberty was not only outside civic Jurisdiction; it was also exempt from the bishop's taxes, and had its own legislation — canon law.

The Liberty's most imposing building is the former **Deanery** rebuilt and much enlarged 1472-1498 by Dean Gunthorpe. In true Wells style it has a substantial gatehouse, plain but dignified, giving access to a spacious courtyard, around which the house is built, in two main blocks, each with halls and chambers.

In a guest chamber with an oriel window slept King Henry VII on October 1st, 1497, when he came to Wells with an army of 10,000 in pursuit of Perkin Warbeck. The large sash windows facing the Cathedral Green are late seventeenth century and possibly by Sir Christopher Wren. The old deanery is owned and occupied by the Diocesan Board of Finance and the Dean lives in the East Liberty, nearby. The Deanery was known as 'The Dean's House'.

Probably few Wells' residents realise what a very fine building the old Deanery is, but it is currently under restoration and when completed will be open to parties of the public by appointment. Among

41

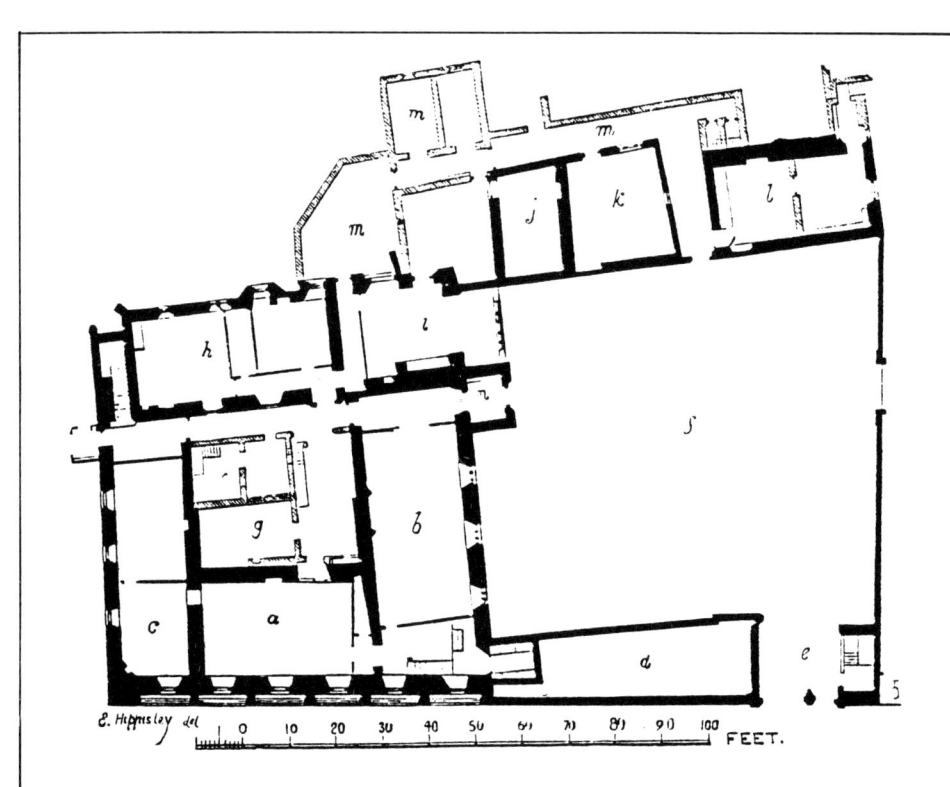

Ground-plan of the Deanery.

a. Hall or Chamber on the Ground Floor, now the Dining Room.
b. Elizabethan or later Hall, either added or rebuilt.
c. Site of Kitchen, now the Dean's Study; the Buttery and Pantry were between this and the Servants' Staircase at the corner; the State Staircase was external, at the same corner.
d. Offices along the wall of the Outer Court, under a terrace.
e. Gate-house.
f. Outer Court.
g. Inner Court, partly built over by modern buildings.
h, i. Offices under the Great Hall.
j, k. Cellars or Store-rooms.
l. Store-rooms, but having rather the appearance of having been a Chapel.
m, m, m. Modern Offices.
n. Porch.

Plan of The Deanery (reproduced with acknowledgement from J.H.Parker's The Architectural Antiquities of Wells)

the fascinating relics of medieval life are the extra handrails for children in the spiral staircases. In the garden, near the base of the tower, is now a small garden of herbs, tended by Diocesan staff, commemorating Dean Turner (1551-4 and 1560-8), the author of *A New Herbal* and known as 'The Father of English Botany'.

East of the old deanery is the **Wells Museum**, built in the sixteenth century as the Chancellor's house, but passing into lay ownership after two chancellors had lived there. It was considerably altered in the eighteenth and nineteenth centuries. In 1930 it was acquired by the Wyndham Trust and has since been the Wells Museum, with some financial support from the City Council. The Museum collection of local historical and archaeological artifacts had been founded by H.E. Balch in 1883 and was originally in the cathedral's west cloister. As previously noted, the embalmed first swan to ring the moat bell for food is among the exhibits, and there is an excellent local history reference library upstairs, open on announced days about twice a week.

Next again, to the east, is the **old archdeaconry** — the building which today houses the Music Department of the Cathedral School. This was the residence of the Archdeacon of Wells until 1555 when the abrupt departure of Archdeacon Polydor Virgil for criticising Henry VIII caused the house to be appropriated and sold. (In the seventeenth century one of the bishops set aside a canonical house on the south of Market Place for an archdeaconry, but it was later, in 1779, sold to the Corporation. The Archdeacon did not need to live in Wells, as his duties took him around the parishes). Much of Virgil's *Anglicae Historiae Libri XXVI* — a valuable source of information on early Tudor days — was probably written here.

Of the original house little remains beyond the fifteenth century great hall, but it has a distinguished Victorian façade, with oriel window and stairway turret. From 1890, for over eighty years, the building served as Wells Theological College; but the college merged with Salisbury in 1971 and the Wells students transferred there — a cultural and spiritual loss to the city and neighbourhood.

Just beyond the old archdeaconry St Andrew's Street is crossed by the Chain Bridge from the cathedral, and immediately beyond is the entrance to **Vicar's Close**. This is one of the showpieces of Wells, the oldest complete street in Europe. But although today it is a pedestrian

Vicars' Close, looking north. By the device of slightly narrowing the north end, an impression of greater length in perspective was created.

thoroughfare, Vicars' Close was laid out as an elongated quadrangle, for a fourteenth century college. The double row of once-identical tall-chimneyed dwellings was started in 1348 by Bishop Ralph (1329-63) to accommodate the vicars who deputised for the canons (*see* chapter 1).

For the previous two hundred years the vicars had had to find their own accommodation in the city. Since they had to attend eight[10] services a day, and an exemplary life was expected of them, Bishop Ralph determined to provide a college close to the Cathedral, where they would be at hand for the Chancellor's lectures, would enjoy a guaranteed standard of living, and be removed from the temptations of secular life. A hall for meals[11], with kitchen and bakehouse at the south end completed the facilities until Bishop Bubwith (1407-25) built the chapel at the north end and added walled gardens and gates to the houses, *c.* 1415. The **Chain Gate Bridge**, sanctioned by the Dean & Chapter in 1459 during Bekynton's episcopae, provided a convenient route between Close and Cathedral without access to the town.

Chain Gate Bridge, St Andrew's Street

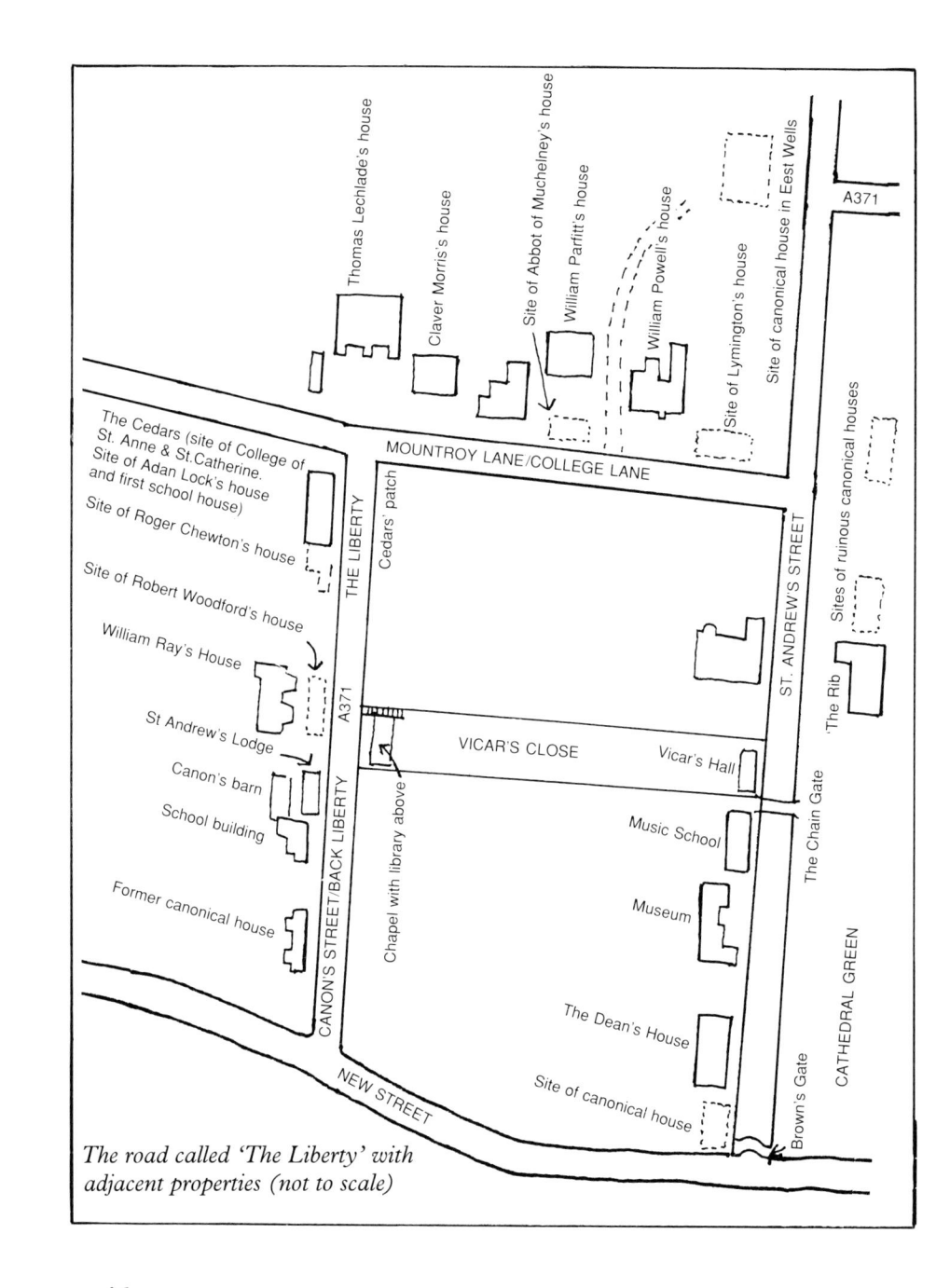

The road called 'The Liberty' with adjacent properties (not to scale)

THE LIBERTY

Discipline was tightened by entrusting the Keys of the Close Gate to the two senior vicars. Richard Pomeroy, a vicar during Henry VIII's reign, and evidently more affluent than most, added the eastern end of the hall which extends over the vaulted gateway, at his own expense. There were originally forty-two houses of two rooms each — one up, one down. When the number of canons and vicars was reduced after the Reformation, some of the houses were combined. Today there are only twelve single houses, but fourteen doubles.

The Library chamber over the chapel was the last addition to the Close, by Bishop Bekynton, *c.* 1460. At various times in the present century the residents have included theological students (till 1971), Cathedral dignitaries[12] and retired clergy, but the Close continuously provides the homes of the vicars choral, — the modern, lay successors of the minor canons who first came to live here in the late fourteenth century, and the Cathedral vergers.

The last building eastward in St. Andrews Street is **Tower House**, now in lay ownership but historically Dean & Chapter property. From the sixteenth century, if not earlier, this was the residence of the Precentor. The south end of the house has fourteenth century remains. The sixteenth century tower, at the north end, has rooms only on the top two floors, the remainder being filled with the stairway.

On the opposite side of St. Andrew's Street is a house called **'The Rib'** which has recently been sold into private lay ownership. It had formerly served as the home of the Cathedral School's headmaster, and until 1971 as the Theological College principal's residence. It is a fifteenth century building and the only survivor of five houses (three east of the Cathedral and two in St. Thomas Street) which were in the gift of the bishop, and had been known colloquially as 'the bishop's ribs'. Its back garden extends to the pond of the wells and is in the shadow of the Lady Chapel.

Other significant buildings are in the right-angled road simply known as 'The Liberty' but until recently as North Liberty and East Liberty and in earlier times as Back Liberty and Mounteroy Lane respectively.

Moving east from the junction with New Street, the first house of interest in North Liberty is named **'Polydor'** and is noticeable for the sea-shell hood, with cherubs, over the front entrance. This feature dates from *c.* 1700 when the house was largely rebuilt, but this is a fifteenth century canonical house, as the exterior buttresses and interior arch-braced roof confirm. When the 'Quirister's House' by the cathedral's west cloister became dilapidated, the organist of the time was allocated this house in 1870, and it remained the organist's residence till 1970. It is now used by the Cathedral School.

East of the back of Poloydor is the **Canon's Barn**, an Early English style medieval-aisled building much rebuilt in Victorian times, and now incorporated in the Cathedral School. It was a tithe barn of the Dean and Chapter.

In front of the barn, and largely concealing it from the road, is **St. Andrew's Lodge**, deriving its name from the carving between the arch and lintel of the front door. Although it has been used in the present century as a canonical house, it was built by local philanthropist Philip Hedges in 1713 to accommodate a charity school for boys, under the Barkham, Hickes and Hedges' Foundation. Its counterpart was a girls' school meeting in a Chamberlain Street almshouse; and these two institutions became known as the Wells Blue Schools. The boys at St. Andrew's Lodge seem to have been as rowdy as most, as complaints about the noise they created were frequent until the school moved to Portway! St. Andrew's Lodge is now part of the Cathedral School.

The next house to the east, set well back from the road, is in lay ownership, and known as **William Ray's house** after its first owner. It replaced an older, canonical house which was the Treasurer's house on at least two occasions, and is known to have sustained damage during the Civil War. Much of its stone is no doubt incorporated in the present house.

On the corner between the Liberty and College Road stands a large mansion named **'The Cedars'**, which today is the administrative centre of the Cathedral School. This is one of the most historic sites in Wells. In the early thirteenth century three houses stood here, — one the home of Adam Lock, master mason of the Cathedral during the building of the Nave. This house, in 1235, became the original Cathedral Grammar School and it is remarkable that the school is now back on its original site after a lapse of centuries. Here in 1400 was built the **College of St. Anne and St. Catherine**, by the executors of Bishop Ralph (1329-63).

The Bishop had wished to accommodate within the Liberty the chantry priests. These were chaplains who said masses for the deceased

'The Cedars' — once home of the Tudways, now part of Wells Cathedral School.

at chantry chapels in the Cathedral endowed for the purpose. They had been living in lodging around the town and the Bishop provided in his will that they should be formed into a college and have a more disciplined life, as had been provided for the vicars choral. The new college building almost certainly incorporated the former Charity school building, and is commemorated by the name of College Road.

With the dissolution of chantries in 1547 the college was closed and the building later purchased by Charles Tudway of Wells who replaced it with the present mansion, The Cedars. (This name derives from the plantation[13] of Cedar Trees immediately opposite, across the road. Each of the cedars, including one at the rear of the house, was planted by successive eldest sons on their twenty-first birthday). The Chantry Priests' college remained standing for some years behind 'The Cedars' until it was eventually taken down — a loss to Wells of one of its most historic builidngs. From 'The Cedars' the roadway turns sharply south to meet St.Andrew's Street, and here are more houses of interest.

Nearest to the corner is a house built at the turn of fifteenth and sixteenth centuries, and now incorporated into the Cathedral School, with the name **'De Salis'**. It replaced an earlier house on the site which had been granted by a lay owner to two vicars, and was known for over two hundred years as 'the house of Lechlade', after one of them. Later it became a canonical residence until 1547. After the Restoration it reverted to canonical use and was known as 'Bisse's House' after Canon Philip Bisse (1585-1607), who bequeathed it to the Chapter.

Next to the south is a seventeenth century house which replaced a former canonical residence. It is known as **Claver Morris' House**, after a prominent Wells citizen who lived here as a tenant of the Dean & Chapter. As with most of the other buildings in the Liberty, it is now part of the flourishing Cathedral School.

We can see, therefore, that although The Liberty may appear to a casual visitor as just a pleasant locality with rather large houses, it is in fact an area full of interest, which has essentially changed little for hundreds of years; and composed mostly of fifteenth century dwellings, although sash windows have long replaced the mullioned windows of days gone by, and the original stones are hidden by weather cladding.

More fifteenth century work would still be evident had the Chapter maintained a more rigorous control over their properties. Often the residents, usually allowed a life tenure, did not keep them in good repair and were sometimes permitted to move into another house which might happen to be vacant, and then in turn failed to maintain that one. They were also allowed to sub-let and sometimes did so to lay persons, and without any binding agreement about maintenance. Canonical houses in the gift of the Bishop seem to have been more tightly controlled, but many of the chapter houses fell into disrepair and had to be rebuilt.

6 HIGH STREET and VICINITY

Wells High Street is first mentioned in records as early as 1228, and in 1368 is referred to as 'Great Street'. Later it was sometimes known as 'Cheap Street' on account of its market stalls. Although narrow at the east (Market Place) end, the street perceptibly widens from the Star Hotel westwards; and in the sixteenth century the centre of the roadway here was taken up daily by the stalls of butchers and other purveyors, extending as far as the junction with Broad Street, and known as Middle Row[14]. Over these stalls, presumably on pillars like the Exchequer in Market Place, was the **Linen Hall**, a room for conducting the sale of linen cloth. This was rebuilt in 1551.

From the east end the first site of interest is that now occupied by the NatWest Bank. Here, in the fourteenth century, stood the Crystesham Inn, named after its owner, Nicholas Crytesham, M.P. for Wells. Bishop Ralph Erghum (1388-1400) acquired the this building as a temporary accommodation for the chantry priests before the college of St. Anne and St. Catherine (*see* last chapter) was completed. The building later reverted to an inn, and was known as 'The George'. In 1854 it was sold by the Ecclesiastical Commissioners to Stuckey's Banking Company, and was pulled down in 1858 to make way for the building we see today, which later became the National Provincial Bank. The frontage of the building is a repeat, in modern idiom, of its predecessor's gothic façade.

Next door is the Gateway (former International) supermarket. On this site in the sixteenth century stood the Katheryne Whele Inn. It was Dean & Chapter property and Sherwin Bailey tells us (*Wells Manor of Canon Grange*: Alan Sutton, 1985) that it extended 290 feet back from the High Street. In 1875 a confectioner's shop and a bakehouse stood on the site.

'NatWest' on the site of the Crystesham Inn, one-time home of the chantry priests.

High Street, 'perceptibly widens from the Star Hotel westwards'; here stood 'The Shambles' of Middle Row.

No. 13, now the premises of Mackays' boutique, is another site thoroughly researched by Sherwin Bailey. Here, in 1350, were two shops with solars over them, owned by William de Chelworth. The site was developed to include a barton (smallholding) and a garden. At the rear were two houses on the bank of the bishop's millstream. All became dilapidated and vacant until restored by John Hillacre to become a brush factory. John Berry's brush and patten factory traded here from the mid-nineteenth century and were in business until the 1920's.

Here **Guardhouse Lane** intervenes, leading to **Bell Close**. This was formerly Horse Lane, and the corner building, now occupied by the Co-operative fashion shop, is on the site of the ancient Christopher Inn or Novum Hospitium of the vicars choral before the formation of the college of Vicars' Close. The inn was afterward known as Somerset House. As such, it had a pillared porch spanning the pavement, of which no trace now exists. The name 'Guardhouse Lane' is said to date from the Napoleonic Wars. French soldiers of Massena's army, taken prisoner during the Peninsular campaign are said to have been imprisoned in the city guardhouse here — on the west side. This tall building was in use as Fry's grain storehouse early this century, but was later incorporated into Woolworths as their Garden department.

Another lane — **Mill Street** — leaves the High Street a few yards further on, at a point known almost into living memory as Jacob's Well. Here, outside what is now Mary's dress shop, stood the Town Pump (notice the wider pavement). In the late fourteenth century, today's Mill Street was called Mullane or Le Mulle Lane. By the late eighteenth century it had become Millpond Lane. Mill Street bridges St. Andrew's stream, which drove the Bishop's Mills and today there are two adjacent dwellings at this point named The Old Mill House. However there seems to be no documentary evidence that the bishop had a mill at this site.

Broad Street[15] diverges to the south-west just beyond the site of 'Jacob's Well', and High Street continues in reduced width to join St. Cuthbert Street. At the junction with Queen Street stands the City Arms Inn, an entrance sign proclaiming 'City gaol in Tudor times'. In fact, inn and gaol existed together from the sixteenth century. This was the gaol granted to the citizens by Elizabeth I, distinct from the bishop's prison. The cells can still be seen, although much of the prison

HIGH STREET and VICINITY

The City Arms — access to gaol cells is under the low roof.

and a fifteen by fourteen feet room adjoining, known as the Burgesses' Chamber, were rebuilt after a city fire in 1746.

Queen Street links High Street with Priory Road and Broad Street at Queen Cross, though this name for the junction is rarely used today. Simes' map shows that a stone cross stood here in the mid-eighteenth century. The origin of the names 'Queen Street' and 'Queen Cross' is not known, but the probability is a commemoration of the visit of Richard II and Anne of Bohemia, soon after their marriage in 1382. They were benefactors of the city and on this visit jointly donated one mark to the civic funds. The earliest reference to Queen Street is in 1440.

On the north side of High Street, older residents and visitors may recall that the site of Dixon's, at the corner with Union Street, was in the 1910s & '20s a cafe nicknamed locally, 'the poor man's restaurant'. It was run by Mr. McKenzie, the then Bishop's gardener, with his wife and daughter and was noted for its excellent but inexpensive fare.

The **Wells Public Library**, on the west side of Union Street, moved from Market Place into these purpose-built premises in 1968.

55

The design of the building earned a Civic Trust award that year.

The **King's Head**, now a Courage house, is one of Wells's oldest taverns. Reputedly built *c.*1320, tradition says it was first a hostel and refectory for the cathedral builders. This inn deserves more than passing notice. There is a central fourteenth century bar, to which galleries have been restored, and a 'market room' on the first floor. The King commemorated would seem to have been King John.

The **Star Inn**, a fifteenth century tavern, has been trading on these same premises for nearly five hundred years, its first mention in records being in 1513. During 1990 the interior is to be remodelled and the courtyard re-roofed.

Queen Cross.

Sadler Street, showing the White Hart.

Brown's Gate

HIGH STREET and VICINITY

On the west side of Sadler Street, running north from High Street, stands the **Swan Hotel**. The Swan, known for most of its long life as 'an inn' rather than an hotel, is first referred to in city records in 1422 (seven years after Agincourt) when the Corporation rented it to John and Isabel Pury for 46/8d a year. By the end of Elizabeth I's reign the annual rent had risen to £4. The Swan was largely rebuilt in the sixteenth century, flooded (according to Claver Morris' *Diary of a West Country Physician*) in the eighteenth century and extensively altered in almost every century. (A sixty-five feet dining room was a nineteenth century feature). For years the Swan was the banquetting hall of the mayor and commonalty, and was the venue of a feast in honour of a visit by Queen Anne of Denmark in 1613. In the coaching era it was a major Posting House and later, when virtually all visitors arrived by rail, the Swan ran its own conveyance to collect passengers from the three railway stations.

The **White Hart** was formerly the Hart's Head — its name was changed in 1700.

Sadler Street's principal architectural feature is **Brown's Gate** (otherwise Barons Gate, and sometimes known as 'the Dean's eye'). This has been less well preserved than other Wells gatehouses, and bears the scars of time. In 1841 the Corporation were considering its demolition, but the Dean and Chapter would not consent. Until the mid-seventies, one-way vehicular traffic used the archway to enter Sadler Street.

St Cuthbert's Church from Priest Row.

7 PLACES OF WORSHIP

St. Cuthbert's Parish Church, which has given its name to the street in which it stands, is the largest parish church in Somerset. Its origin is not known, but the discovery, around 1900, of a Norman pillar piscina (in the Lady Chapel) indicates that there was a church here in the twelfth century. St Cuthbert was a highly esteemed Saxon saint in the days of King Alfred, so it may be that a church — probably of wood — stood on this site by the end of the ninth century.

What was perhaps the third church on the site was erected in the thirteenth century and this was the nucleus, many times altered and enlarged, of the magnificent church we see today. The most important remains of the thirteenth century church are the piers and arches of the nave — there are seven bays. There were wholesale restorations, amounting to rebuilding in the fourteenth and fifteenth centuries, so that the church today is almost purely Perpendicular in style.

In the thirteenth century form, St. Cuthbert's was cruciform, with a central tower at the crossing of the transepts. This central tower survived until the 1560s. The lofty western tower[16] (height 153 feet) so admired today began building in 1410 and was twelve feet distant from the west wall of the nave, which then had only six bays. St. Cuthbert's therefore possessed two towers for well over a hundred years. The westernmost bay of the nave, joining the western tower to the main building, was completed in the late fifteenth century.

Also about this time the Perpendicular clerestory was erected above the nave arches and the magnificent flat roof over the nave aisle. It is likely that this work destabilised the central tower by overloading its piers, for the tower crashed in 1561 or 2 and collections were held in the town to meet the repair. The decision was then taken not to rebuild the tower, but to raise the chancel arch and bring all the space under the tower into the nave. The clerestory wall was therefore extended eastward to meet the chancel arch. These changes gave St. Cuthbert's the appearance it has today.

An interesting feature of the church is the extension of the north and side aisles beyond the nave, almost to the end of the chancel, and this provided the space for a number of subsidiary chapels, as in a cathedral. The side chapels on the north side are:-

Holy Trinity Chapel — St. Cuthbert's has always been the civic church of Wells and this chapel traditionally was for the Mayor and Corporation and contained their official seats (now in the nave). Today it is the chapel of the Mothers Union branch, and is reserved for private prayer.

St. Catherine's Chapel — occupies the original north transept. On its east wall is a thirteenth century reredos which was terribly mutilated by iconoclasts in the sixteenth century, and plastered over, but was rediscovered in 1848, and restored as far as possible.

Chapels on the south side are:-

St. Cuthbert's Chapel — has a fifteenth century panelled ceiling which has long been concealed under plaster and was only recently rediscovered and cleaned. In this chapel can be seen, in the north-west pier, the remains of the doorway which formerly led, spirally, to the one-time rood loft.

The Lady Chapel — this was first a chantry founded by a fourteenth century mayor of Wells named Tanner, and is still alternatively known as 'Tanner's Chapel'. It contains one of the church's greatest prizes in the 'Jesse' reredos, which covers the east wall. It portrays the descent of Israel's royal line from Jesse, father of King David.

St. Cuthbert's can be summarised as a perpendicular rebuilding of an Early English parish church, occupying the site of a much earlier Saxon oratory. But it is so much more: an exceptionally fine church full of architectural and historical treasures, on a spot sanctified by dedication to the worship of God from time immemorial.

The church is open daily and beautifully illustrated guide books are on sale, which give full information on the building and its history.

St Thomas's Parish Church — East Wells, physically separated from St. Cuthbert's by the area of the Liberty and cathedral complex, was for long largely inhabitated by the poorer citizens, and indeed

St Thomas' Church — Teulon's steeple dominates east Wells.

became something of a slum, known locally by the disparaging name 'Turkey' — the habitation of infidels. Dr. Richard Jenkyns, Dean of Wells 1845-54, was much concerned about this and made plans for the erection of a church in the area. He died in 1854, but his widow, Troth Jenkyns, saw that his wishes were fulfilled.

The foundation stone was laid in 1856 and St. Thomas' church was consecrated the following year. The architect was S.S. Teulon, now recognised as a leading Victorian architect, and he designed the church in the Gothic Revival 'Geometrical' style. The steeple is a landmark for the district, and rises to 145 feet; the tower being surmounted by statues of the four evangelists at the base of the spire. Nave and chancel have a steep arch-braced collar roof. The south aisle was not added till later and increased the seating capacity to 592, while the choir vestry dates from 1926.

Inside, the piers of the gothic arches deserve notice. Those on the north side have lias stone barrels, based on and capped by Doulting stone. The carved capitals are all different and show vines, fig leaves, holly, oak, and other leaves and tendrils. On the south side the columns are less ornamented. The coloured stone around the arches is thought to be Ham Stone, and is typical of Teulon's 'chromatic brickwork' — one of that srchtect's 'trademarks'.

The chancel is apsidal, and the walls of the apse bear not only the Creed, Ten Commandments and Lord's Prayer (as enjoined in Tudor times but commonly found in nineteenth century churches) but also texts from the Epistles and the Words of Institution from the Book of Common Prayer. The choir stalls and communion rails have fine brass and hand-wrought iron work.

The stained glass windows on the north side have been restored with their original glass; the windows on the south side were similar till 1979, when, being in poor condition, they were reglazed with clear glass to lighten the building. The East Windows were given by the fellows of Balliol College Oxford, in commemoration of Dean Jenkyns, who had formerly been Master of Balliol.

The pulpit and font are thought to have been made elsewhere to Teulon's design; they are not cut from local stone. The organ by Hill's of London, dates from the early twentieth century and was rebuilt and enlarged in 1955. It has a pinewood case, and richly decorated pipes. The Lady Chapel was furnished in 1930 and renovated in 1979. It is

PLACES OF WORSHIP

regularly used for weekday services.

Dean Jenkyns, whose concern for the spiritual welfare of East Wells inspired the building of St. Thomas', has not been forgotten — nor his widow, who brought his dreams to fruition. In addition to the east windows already noted, a window in the south aisle of the chancel commemorates Mrs Jenkyns, and depicts St. Thomas, with the spear with which he was killed, and a carpenter's square (for he is the patron saint of all builders). On either side of the window are two carved stone heads, presumed to be of Dean and Mrs Jenkyns.

Ebenezer United Reformed Church — the present building was erected in 1827 but the history of its worshipping community goes back to 1750, when the local Independent Baptists took over a former Presbyterian meeting house in East Wells. A dwelling on the west side of Grove Lane (now Union Street) was acquired and altered to form a church and a small day school, its garden becoming a graveyard, and was opened in 1817. The present larger church, with vestry and meeting-rooms, covers a part of the former graveyard. The dedication was 'Ebenezer'.

In 1917 the Wells Congregational Church united with them, with the arrangement that the more modern Baptist building should be used solely, and that ministers should be appointed alternately from the two denominations. The Congregational Church, standing a few yards to the south, had been built at the expense of Mrs Clement Tudway in 1787 and enlarged the following year. A caretaker's cottage and garden were acquired in 1828.

The Seager Hall (commemorating the Congregational minister Rev. G. W. Seager) was built in 1902, and now has access to the United Church. From 1917-21 the Congregational Church lay disused. In World War II it became a WVS community centre, and since then has served as a garage-cum-petrol station, a bakery, and now houses a restaurant and a furnishings shop.

The United Church has a simply-furnished, dignified interior, with a four foot font recessed in front of the pulpit, and a 2 manual Griffin and Stroud organ, restored by Osmond's.

Wells Methodist Church — the Methodist chapel in Southover occupies a site which has been hallowed for over eight hundred years, for until the Reformation there stood here a wayside chapel dedicated to St. Thomas a Becket. Dating from about 1200, it owed its origin beyond doubt to the nationwide semi-idolatrous veneration of the archbishop after his murder in 1170. Henry VIII's antiquary John Leland refers to the chapel in 1541 in the past tense, and local historians have variously claimed evidence of its destruction in 1535 or 1547.

In 1704 the site became the property of the Sevior family of Bristol, who built and endowed a meeting-house for Protestant dissenters, with a small burial ground adjacent. By 1740 it was in use by the Prestbyterians, but it would seem that John Wesley (1703-91) probably preached here on occasions as guest of the Seviors. By 1838 the chapel had come under the formal jurisdiction of the Methodist Church, who rebuilt and enlarged it.

The Ecclesiastical Census for 1851 gives the seating capacity as 370, but this would appear a wildly optimistic figure. In 1865 further enlargement took place, and the church was given its present Doric façade. It was again enlarged in 1878, when the re-opening was conducted by Rev.T.B. Stephenson, founder of the National Childrens Home and Orphanage. A vestry was added in 1920. A major refurbishment took place in 1988, at a cost of £168,000. Today there is a flourishing church life and a community roll of three hundred.

The Elim Church — the Elim community began their work in Wells in 1934, and their founder, George Jeffreys, addressed a large gathering in the Town Hall the following year. In 1937 a house in Chamberlain Street which had been in use as temporary convent by Carmelite nuns was purchased for an Elim tabernacle by the Hodges family of Easton. Extensive alterations were made, to the designs of architect R.O. Stiles. This is the Elim church in use today, and the opening ceremony of 28th July 1937 was performed by Pastor J. Smith of Portsmouth. As seen from the roadway, the right-handed (eastern) part of the building is now in use as offices of the Care-Gomm Society: the left-hand (western) part forms the Church, which extends about thirty yards to the north and can accommodate about one hundred and fifty persons.

St Joseph and St Theresa Roman Catholic Church — the work of the Roman Catholic Church in Wells began when a community of

Carmelite nuns at Plymouth moved to Wells in 1875 at the suggestion of the Roman Catholic Bishop Clifford, who personally found them a home. The community took possession of 'The Vista' in Chamberlain Street on 13th July, 1875 and the First Papal Mass since the Reformation was celebrated by Bishop Clifford three days later, the Feast of Our Lady of Mt. Carmel. The Bishop used a chalice donated to the community by His Holiness Pope Pius IX.

In 1877 the foundation stone of the Church of St. Joseph and St. Theresa was laid in the convent grounds, and opened on 15th October. The façade was copied from a church in Normandy. The nephew of one of the nuns, named Mercer, contributed £1,300 to the construction. The completion of the church was taken in hand in 1888, with the building of the Sanctuary, and a new choir for the nuns. All costs were met by the Carmelite community. A house in Chamberlain Street was acquired for a presbytery in 1924.

The heavy traffic in Chamberlain Street in modern times deprived the community of the peace and quiet desirable for prayer and meditation, and the convent was closed in 1972 when the nuns moved to Darlington. The east end containing the nuns' living quarters was separated and sold for conversion into flats, named 'Carmelite House': the west end was remodelled to provide a church porch on the ground floor, with a youth room over, the convent chapel being opened into the church as a transept. The departure of the nuns[17] was a cultural and spiritual loss to the city rather than a social one, as they were a closed order and their duties were not secular but exclusively devotional .

8 THE PRIORY OF ST. JOHN and ALMSHOUSES

St John's Priory — In medieval times there were many travellers on foot, among them pedlars with wares of every kind, merchant's agents arranging deals or transport of goods, pilgrims making for a shrine, and mendicants seeking charity. The heydey of the inn was yet to come, and in any case many travellers were in no position to pay for their board, and some were in need of medical care. The Church accepted a responsibility for hospitality toward travellers but its ability to respond to their needs varied. The abbeys and large monasteries had considerable resources and ample accommodation but this was not the case with the bishops and secular cathedrals. Here, buildings we should describe as hostels, but then called hospitals, would be established by the bishop, or the chapter, or wealthy lay people, for the benefit of the poorer, disadvantaged wayfarers. By the thirteenth century, such institutions were to be found in all cathedral cities, staffed by friars or by brethren adhering to some recognised Order or rule of life, but who were not necessarily monks.

Such was the case at Wells, where Bishop Jocelyn (a native of the city) and his brother Hugh, who was archdeacon, between them founded the hospital of St. John about the year 1230 and appointed a Prior to be the Master in charge. It was dedicated to St. John the Baptist, and its staff belonged to the order of St. Augustine. This priory, of which only a fragment remains today, occupied a rectangle of land between the present Priory Road, St. John Street and Southover.

The bishop's mill stream passed through the grounds and the buildings must have comprised a chapel, a refectory and kitchen, dormitory for the brethren who formed the staff, and acccommodation — probably basic — for the wayfarers. Whereas almshouses, which

THE PRIORY OF ST. JOHN

came later, catered for the poor of the town itself, St. Johns existed to serve travellers and wayfarers, and to care for any who fell ill while lodging there or passing through the city. The Prior had his own lodging, five minutes walk distant, in Sadler Street, on the south side of the Swan Inn and next to it. Thomas Holmes (*Wells and Glastonbury*, 1908) lists seventeen of the priors, between 1228 and 1539.

In 1231 the Bishop bestowed on the Prior the advowson (right to appoint incumbents) of the living of Evercreech. This may have represented power in a small measure, but it was income that the hospital needed. Shortly after, the priory was endowed by a prominent Wells citizen, William de la Withy, with five houses — one known to have been in Tucker Street — and several acres of land in the city. But St. John's was always underfunded, and this led to dependence on endowments with 'strings attached', *i.e.* endowments in respect of prayers or masses for the departed, which had the effect of using the hospital chapel as a chantry, with priests attached. This led to the

All that remains of the Priory of St John. The interior has substantial medieval remains.

hospital's suppression at the Reformation, when it was deemed to fall within the scope of the Act for the Dissolution of chantries. The axe fell in 1539, and prior Richard Clarkson surrendered that year to the King's commissioners, receiving a compensatory pension of £12 per annum.

Peter, the first prior, had built a mill at Hilemore, to benefit the hospital financially, but was soon in trouble on this account. In a document now preserved in the Wells Chapter records, he binds himself never again to interfere with the rights of the bishop's mills.

The site[18] of the priory is now occupied by St John's Court, Priory Road Post Office, numbers 3 and 5 Priory Road, the 'Priory of St. John' dwelling house (the only authentic remains of the hospital), the cottages of Priory Place and some restored houses in Southover. After the Dissolution, the land changed hands more than once, but eventually came into the possession of the Sherston family. The construction of Priory Road in 1800 (formerly a narrow lane) was probably the first serious encroachment on the priory site. In 1812 Mr. Peter Sherston granted the southern side for the erection of St. Cuthbert's Church 'Central School', founded by Bishop Beadon. Holmes records that as late as 1858 a fourteenth century house was still standing, which had clearly formed part of the priory, and this house was also later donated by Mr. Sherston, whereupon it was demolished to enlarge the school.

The original staffing of the hospital had been a prior (as Master) and ten brethren. In 1439 there were only two brethren assisting Prior Cousin, but in 1445 the number had risen to five, under Prior Vle.

The private dwelling in St. John Street today, which keeps alive the priory name, is believed to have been the living quarters of the medieval brethren. Built into an interior wall of St. John's Court no. 5 is an Early English period doorway surviving from the Priory.

St. John's Priory was for wayfarers. It was many years later that provision was made for the poor and elderly of the city. Today Wells almshouses are among the most picturesque dwellings in the city. The first to be built was the Bubwith almshouse in Chamberlain Street.

Bubwith Almshouse — This building was the benefaction of Bishop Nicholas Bubwith (1407-24) and erected on the south side of Beggar Street, as that part of Chamberlain Street was then known. Originally a one-storey building with a Chapel at the east end and a hall at the

ALMSHOUSES

Bubwith Almshouse, showing the one-time Guildhall at the west end.

west, a central corridor gave access to twelve chambers, or rather cubicles. A first floor was added later over this corridor, increasing the accommodation to twenty-four. It was provided that the inmates should be poor men and women of the burgesses of the city. Patronage, in respect of admissions to vacancies, was shared between the Dean & Chapter and Mayor and Commonalty. In 1466 a chaplain was endowed, but he was also a chantry priest, using the chapel for masses.

The hall at the west end was used for three hundred years as the Guildhall of Wells, in addition to being the inmates' common room and the Board room for the trustees' meetings. The Corporation eventually gave up use of the hall in 1784. It contains a large oak chest, with three locks and keys, provided under the Statutes of the Hospital which were drawn up by Dean Carent in 1454 and sanctioned by no less than Archbishop Stafford, previously Bishop of Bath and Wells. Over the centuries additions to the foundation have been made.

The Still Almshouses, 'for six poor and decayed tradesmen of the city', were erected between the Bubwith building and churchyard in

1614 — the gift of Bishop John Still (1593-1608) and his son Nathaniel. A tablet recording this is over the door of each dwelling.

The Bricke Almshouses — In 1688 a Wells woollen draper, Walter Bricke, provided in his will for the maintenance of 'four poor burgesses not less than fifty years of age, who shall have resided for 7 years previously in Wells.' The Bricke almshouses were also built south of the Bubwith building and next to the Still houses. They are distinguished by four Jacobean canopied stone seats, facing the churchyard. In 1771 Bishop Willes (1743-73) gave the sum of £1200 to support the poor of the city, thereby increasing the accommodation to admit four more men.

Llewellyn Almshouses — Henry Llewellyn of Wells bequeathed £1600 to four senior masters of the city to purchase a site and build almshouses for ten elderly women, each to have a parlour and bedroom and a small plot of garden. His trustees acquired a site on the east side of Priest's Row; this charity has always been managed by the Mayor and Corporation.

Harper Almshouses — This is on the north side of Chamberlain Street, and is marked by an inscribed stone tablet let into the wall. Accommodation, under the will of Archibald Harper in 1711 was for 'five poor decayed woolcombers' who had served their apprenticeships in Wells. In 1732, when the wool trade was in decline, the Bishop decreed that if no 'decayed woolcombers' could be found, any other genuine poor might be considered. The building (on the site of Harper's own dwelling) has five rooms and a common room.

9 SCHOOLS and HOSPITALS

Wells Cathedral School — Wells Cathedral School, by far the longest-established school in the city, can look back on over one thousand years of history. From as early as the tenth century the Cathedral was running two schools, both referred to in the 1140 statutes:- a grammar school the responsibility of the Chancellor, and a song school, the responsibility of the Precentor. The original site of the school is not known, but by the thirteenth century it was in a house in the Liberty presented to the Chancellor by Canon Roger Chewton, chaplain to Bishop Jocelyn. ('The Cedars', centre of the present-day school, covers the site of that medieval building.) Educational training was mainly to qualify for ordination to the ministry. The number of pupils probably did not exceed fifty. The school was displaced when its site, and that of houses on either side, was required by Bishop Erghum (1388-1400) for his new college for chantry priests, and moved first to premises in Tor Street, then to the house 'De Salis' in East Liberty, and eventually over the Cathedral's west cloister.

Meanwhile the equally old, if not older, song school for choristers was being conducted in a T-shaped building near the west cloister, of which only the fragment known as the 'Quiristers' House' remains. The numbers were small — twelve boys altogether, six choristers and six ex-choristers with special duties. Rules for the conduct of the choristers, drawn up in the early fifteenth century, have survived, and include; 'No unlawful or dishonourable or unnatural behaviour be permitted to develop, grow or flourish among the boys, particularly rascally conduct, swearing, lying, brawling, quarrelling, fighting, contention, raucous laughter, jeering or any other unseemly behaviour of this nature.'

In 1547 Edward VI's advisors ordered every cathedral to establish a free grammar school if none already existed, and laid down various conditions, including much increased staff salaries. It seems likely that advantage was taken of this 1547 injunction to unite the two schools, for we know that this took place sometime in the sixteenth century.

In 1851 the Cathedral School and Blue School shared the same headmaster and the St. Andrew's Lodge building in the Liberty. When the Blue School moved to Chamberlain Street, the Cathedral School returned to the West Cloister. This was a low period in the school's fortune, and numbers had fallen to nineteen boys, including fourteen choristers, but this situation improved when in 1899 provision was made in the curriculum for boys to receive either classical or mercantile education.

In 1881 the school moved into the former Chancellor's House (now the Wells Museum) while in 1883 Chancellor Bernard built, at his own expense, new premises in the Liberty which came to be known as the Bernard building, while the Dean & Chapter granted to the school the ancient Canon's Barn and land adjoining.

The modern history of the school really begins with the headmastership of the Rev. A.F. Ritchie, who came in 1924. Ritchie persuaded the Chapter to lease to the school the large Tudway Mansion, 'The Cedars', in place of the old Chancellor's house, and thus the school came to occupy again its thirteenth century site. He also established a Junior School in New Street. Ritchie was succeeded in 1954 by Frank Cummings, who raised teaching staff salaries to conform to the Burnham Scale. He was followed in 1964 by A.K. Quilter, in whose time numerous additions and improvements were made to the school buildings. The re-housing of the Cathedral canons in the late 1960's enabled the Chapter to lease four houses in the Liberty to the school, which now had a long waiting-list for entry, so the extra buildings were soon fully used.

There was a considerable departure from tradition when in Michaelmas 1969, girl pupils were admitted for the first time — to junior forms only in the first instance, so that the boys grew up with them.

In 1970 Wells became one of the four specialist music schools in England. Today Wells Cathedral School has an enviable reputation, and is flourishing with over seven hundred pupils.

Wells Blue School — The Blue School, off Milton Lane, is a

SCHOOLS and HOSPITALS

voluntary controlled comprehensive school with origins in the seventeenth century. Ezekiel Barkham, a wealthy citizen, says in his will dated 22nd Sept. 1641 that during his lifetime he had sold land, which produced £30 a year, for £800, and this he desired put to pious use. His widow established a Charity School for the free education of poor children in Wells. Known first as the Free School of Margaret Barkham, it opened in 1656, with fourteen boy pupils, using the Bubwith almshousechapel as classroom. (The schoolmaster was also Master of the almshouse). The foundation benefitted from bequests and legacies of local people in 1675, 1718 and 1720.

In 1723 the school moved to St. Andrew's Lodge, North Liberty, erected by Philip Hodges of Wells on land owned by the Dean & Chapter. The children of poor parents of Chamberlain Street and New Street were to have priority of places. By the beginning of the eighteenth century there were thirty-four boys and twenty girls. On account of free blue uniforms given to each pupil the school became known as the Blue School, a title formally adopted by 1750.

During the eighteenth century the school was carried on in the North Liberty, when complaints were continually made of the noise created by the boys. Further bequests enabled a new site to be acquired at the south-west corner of Chamberlain Street, when a house named **'Soho'** and its garden were purchased ('Soho' was the password of Monmouth's army in 1685 and the house had been the home of a sympathiser). When the school was later rebuilt, 'Soho' — which had served as the Master's house — was pulled down; but the new redbrick building for the boys bore the name 'Soho' carved on a brick on its western and northern façades. By 1900 there were one hundred pupils plus a further twenty over-fifteen pupil teachers under the Board of Education training scheme. To accomodate these, a new building in stone, distinguished by a 'pagoda' turret, was erected in Portway in 1913. This later became the girls' building. In 1932 the school was classified 'Grammar School' and had 260 pupils. A new block with gymnasium was erected in 1937.

In the 'sixties the school lost its Grammar School status under the scheme for introducing comprehensive education, and was merged with Kennion Road Secondary School into a new comprehensive which today has 1,150 pupils, and since 1965 has been in new premises at Milton Lane to which the 'Soho' stones have been transferred.

The former boys' block is now 'The Little Theatre' — where the Wells Dramatic Society perform frequent plays; the girls' block, which had become a Teachers' Centre, is again used by the school; whilst the erstwhile gymnasium block is the headquarters of Wells Youth Club.

The Keward Schools — Soon after formation of the National Society in London, similar societies were formed throughout the kingdom. The Diocese of Bath and Wells immediately offered to co-operate with the Society, and in August 1812 a meeting was held in Wells to consider action, and find a site for a diocesan school. The Sherston family then gave a surviving building of St. John's Priory for the purpose – which had been in use as a wool factory — to Dean Rider, vicar of St. Cuthbert's, who established a parish school in the old building. This was modified to create a two-room one up, one down school, with the necessary offices, to accommodate three hundred children. This building was completely razed and rebuilt as the Central Schools, in 1858. It was a dignified stone building with gothic windows and a lofty campanile. It was an all-ages school until the 'thirties when the senior children transferred to Kennion Road. Even so, the school was overcrowded for juniors and infants before long, and in 1959 the infants were transferred to a temporary school in a former British Restaurant building adjacent to Clare's Equipment factory, with access from Southover.

In 1977 Somerset Education Authority built a new junior school at Keward, to which the juniors at Priory Road were transferred. The old Central School of 1858 was then sold and has since been converted into dwellings, the campanile being preserved. Today's modern building still bears the name **Central Voluntary Controlled School**, and is a Church of England school with two hundred and thirty children on roll.

The Infants moved from the temporary Southover school in 1981, into another modern school at Keward Walk, which is named **St. Cuthbert's Voluntary Controlled Infants**, and has over one hundred and eighty children on its registers.

The Stoberry Schools — In East Wells the Church pioneered education when St. Thomas' School was built in 1859 by the first vicar of the parish. It was a typical Victorian building, and quite elegant, on

SCHOOLS and HOSPITALS

the north side of St. Thomas Street. This church school catered for scholars of all ages until the 1930s, when there were 230 pupils on the roll. Senior children then transferred to Kennion Road school. St. Thomas' continued as a Primary (junior and infants) school until 1963. In that year Stobbery County Infants School was opened by the Local Education Authority and the St. Thomas' infants transferred there. Twenty years elapsed during which St. Thomas' continued as a voluntary controlled junior school and the County planned a new school as Stoberry Park. **Stoberry Park Junior School** opened in 1973 and St. Thomas' transferred its pupils and closed that same year. The two Stoberrry schools are quite separate entities. Stoberry Park Junior retains close links with St. Thomas Church but is a County School and has about one hundred and eighty six children on roll. The **Stoberry Infants School** includes 'county' in its name and has about one hundred and fifty on roll. The St. Thomas school building has since been demolished and housing development occupies its site.

St Joseph and St Theresa Primary School — The absence of a poor school in Wells providing Roman Catholic religious instruction decided the Carmelite community at Wells convent in 1877 to give up part of their grounds for the purpose. The Duke of Norfolk subscribed £400 for the building of the school, which was erected on the east side of Union Street. In 1887 an Apostoline sister, St. Mary Joseph, who was a certified teacher, took up work at the school and continued teaching there for many years. Later, the Carmelite nuns gave up more of their land for the school to be extended. Increasing numbers necessitated the school hiring an additional classroom at the YMCA hut.

In 1975 new school premises were erected in redbrick at Lovers' Lane, and the juniors transferred there. Union Street remained open for infants till 1981, and was then converted into two cottages.

HOSPITALS

Wells and District Hospital — The Wells and District Hospital will always be known locally as the Cottage Hospital, whatever name is officially bestowed on it by the Health authority.

Two cottages at the top of St. Thomas Street were first converted for hospital use in 1874, and it was twenty years later that these were pulled down and a purpose built hospital erected on their site. Additions to the building were made in 1929 and 1979, when there were three wards, male general, female general and maternity. Over the years the services provided by the hospital have varied according to the policy and requirements of the time, but have included general medical, general surgical, casualty, maternity and geriatric. The bed capacity has never exceeded thirty-six and is currently twenty-eight. An enviable reputation for expert care and friendly atmosphere here has been built up, and although rumours of closure haunt all 'cottage' hospitals perpetually, Wells is high in popular esteem and opposition to any such move would certainly be vigorous.

Mendip Hospital — Although locally regarded as a Wells hospital and recruiting most of its staff from the city, the Mendip Hospital has always served the county area, and in fact is just outside the city boundary of the parish of Horrington. It was built as the County Lunatic Asylum in 1847 and stands in a pleasant and wooded thirty-six acre site, intended originally to accommodate three hundred patients. Further blocks were later added, the name was changed to Mendip Hospital and during the 1950's nearly one thousand patients were being accommodated.

Under the present-day policy of Care in the Community, the hospital will close in March 1991 and, at the time of writing, houses only about one hundred in-patients. The handsome and capacious chapel with a spire was closed a few years ago and replaced by a small chapel in the centre block.

With the hospital's closing now imminent, a range of community-based mental health services are or will be provided in the city, as follows:-

9 Acute Day Places	Rosebank, Bath Rd (later, to Glastonbury)
28 Rehab. Day Places	Priory Park, Glastonbury Road.
25 Acute Beds	" "
18 Acute Day Places	" "
26 Elderly Beds	" "
26 Elderly Day Places	" "
22 Rehab. Beds	Keward House, Keward Estate.

SCHOOLS and HOSPITALS

Priory Hospital — The Priory Hospital in Glastonbury Road was erected in 1838 as the Wells Union Workhouse. (Because of architectural merit it is now a listed building). Under the Poor Law Amendment Act it catered chiefly for the able-bodied poor and for pauper children. By the 1860's these were being gradually replaced by disabled and infirm elderly poor folk, which resulted in the building of a new infirmary block in 1871 by Moore & Perrin. There was also a maternity ward for unmarried mothers.

When the Union and Board of Guardians were abolished in 1930, Somerset County Council changed the name to Wells Public Assistance Institution — later changed again to Rowden's House. In 1933 the casual wards — which admitted vagrants on condition they worked for two nights board and lodging — were closed. The National Health Service took over in 1948 and the upgrading of the hospital began. First renamed Wells Infirmary it became the Priory Hospital in 1961.

Today the hospital has four wards and provides care for the elderly (69 beds). A Day Hospital section, recently opened, can take twelve patients daily. Physiotherapy and Occupational therapy are available both for in-patients and day patients. The number of staff at the hospital is 120.

Sadly, in June 1990, Somerset Health Authority announced the closure of Priory Hospital in 1992.

Street plan of Wells today.

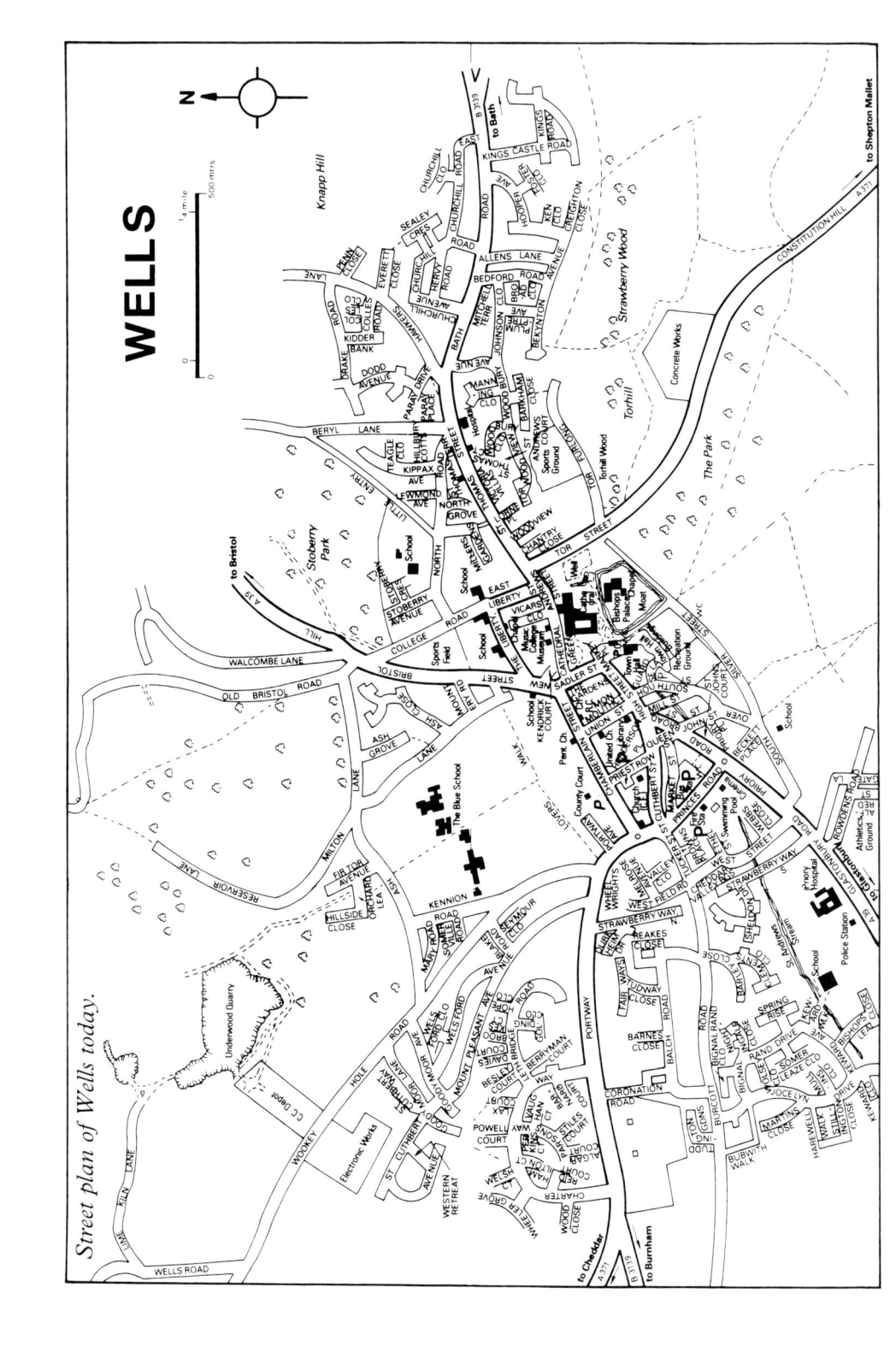

10 ROUND ABOUT WELLS

Fire Station — Wells Fire Station in Princes Road was established in 1937 on the site of a garage purchased by the City Council. The existing Merryweather Albion tender with a Hatfield trailer was then transferred there from Market Place, and a second appliance was acquired – a Dennis tender and pump, at a cost of £150. A siren, first used for air raid warning, was supplied by the Home Office, and mounted on the hose tower. During 1990-91 the building is to be demolished to make way for a Tesco superstore, and a new fire station built off Burcott Road.

Gallows Close, Keward — The long-time traditional place for execution. Judge Jeffrey's 'Bloody Assize' in 1685 condemned ninety-nine men to death, of which nine were hung locally, presumably in this field, although it is thought one or two were hung in the Market Place. Latterly an orchard, Gallows Close was recently acquired for housing development and now bears the name Bishoplea Close.

Judge's Lodging — The fine house where the circuit judges lodged when Wells was an Assize town, can still be seen in New Street. Prior to 1843, judges had been accomodated by prominent citizens, but in that year a trust was set up to acquire and manage a suitable property. First used as the judge's lodging in 1843, and last in 1970, the house has since been converted into flats, but retains the name.

Mermaid Inn, Tucker Street — The Mermaid is a Victorian rebuild of a very old tavern, mentioned in the public records early in the sixteenth century. Until the eighteenth century it was held by the Cordwent family. During the course of alterations in 1854, builder's men uncovered an unsuspected doorway bearing the date 1690.

Park Meadows, Dulcote footpath — The original road to Shepton Mallet went this way until 1207 when Bishop Jocelyn diverted the road to make his palace more private. The meadows were then forested. Park Wood is all that remains of the forest.

Recreation Ground — This was opened on 22nd August 1888 (which the city made a public half-holiday) to commemorate the Golden Jubilee of Queen Victoria. It was Bishop Hervey's suggestion that provision of a recreation ground would make a fitting memorial, and the ground was purchased by public subscription from the Ecclesiastical Commissioners; and in 1897, to mark the Diamond Jubilee, it was transferred to the City Concil. The land consisted of (1) the former conygre of the bishops, with tithe barn, two cottages, gardens and yard, and (2) the field known as Bell Close. A caretaker was appointed with the tenancy of one of the cottages. The barn has since proved a useful venue for social gatherings and meetings. Prime Minister Sir Alec Douglas Home addressed a crowded meeting here in 1964. The one-time conygre has been laid out formally with bandstand and park seats, while Bell Close is used for football and occasional circuses. A German howitzer gun, captured by British Infantry, stood by the **Bishop's Barn** between the wars, displayed on a plinth. As with the Russian gun in the Market Place, it was removed for scrap, early in World War II.

St. Andrew Street and the Duke of Wellington — On the northeast corner of the junction with East Liberty once stood a fourteenth century house named 'La Purihey' (pear orchard). This was once owned by the Wellesley, formerly Wellesleigh family, before they settled in Ireland. One of the Duke of Wellington's titles was 'Baron Dourd of Wellesley in the county of Somerset'.

St. Thomas Street — Formerly named Byestwelles. There were many inns in this street, much patronised by Mendip miners, but none has survived. There were also some prebendal houses, while a number of the smaller dwellings were the property of the Dean & Chapter.

Tor Street — In medieval times the Tor Gate in and out of Wells stood close to the Chilcote Stream (about one hundred yards from the present crossroads), which was crossed by the small Tor Bridge. Over the gate was a private chapel, for which a due of 4d a year was paid to the Bishop. Gate and chapel were ruinous by 1446 and demolished soon after. Today the Chilcote stream passes under Tor Street in a culvert.

Stoberry Park (private) — The surviving part of the Stoberry Estate including the sites of the earlier (pre-1830) and later (rebuilt 1930) Stoberry House. Property of the Davis family to 1778, the Sherstons to 1854, and the Tudways to 1955, when it was demolished. Owned now by the Tudway-Quilters, the estate includes the mansions Beaumont House (let), Stoberry coach-house (let) and Milton Lodge (the family home).

Church of the Good Shepherd — In Southover, but was closed in 1971 and now an architect's office. A 'mission church' of unknown de-

The Bishop's Barn

nomination was built on this site in 1851, and taken over by the Congregationalists, 1857. The Church of the Good Shepherd was built 1907 as a chapel-of-ease to St. Cuthbert's.

Becket Place, Southover — Named after the dedication of the wayside chapel which formerly occupied the site of the Methodist church. Here was a 'very large and handsome tree' which, says Serel, 'had become a meeting-place for the women of the district, who would knit and gossip there'.

Keward House and Mill — The Keward mill and estate were in medieval times the property of the Bishop. In the 1554 will of Thomas Clark, brother of the then bishop, the mill and ground were left to William Gervys, his servant. After Gervys' death, Mr. Parson Fitz-James was to have it. The present day Keward House is nineteenth century and was last used as a residence by the Harris family (owners of Harris Motors) who had purchased it from a farmer named Clark. Today Keward House is a rehabilitation centre linked to Mendip hospital, while the Mill is used as offices.

Wells Cemetery — Opened for burials in the early nineteenth century, but the earliest purchased grave was in 1858. Here is the grave of Mary Simpson, second wife of Earnest Simpson, whose wife Wallis married the abdicated King Edward VIII. This grave had frequent visitors during the showing of the television series 'Mrs Simpson'.

The German airmen killed when their Dornier DO 17Z crashed at Maesbury Ring in October 1943 were buried here until re-interred in the German military graveyard at Cannock Chase in 1967.

Wells Cinemas — The Palace cinema in Priory Road was opened in 1912 by the Collins family to meet the local demand for the new entertainment marvel – the 'Movies'. The building, which had formerly been an auctioneer's saleroom and mineral water factory, was also used for Theatre and Music Hall. 'Talkies' came to the Palace in 1926 and that same year a brick extension was built at the north end, and a handsome glass canopy provided for the queues at the south frontage; seating capacity was about 250. A measure of the prosperity of the cinema in those days was that the Palace's pianist earned more for three evenings work than he did as an articled clerk to solicitors in a six day week!

The Regal Cinema in Princes Road was built in 1934 and owned by Clifton Cinemas until 1984 when it was purchased by three Wells businessmen who formed Somarea Promotions Ltd. Wells had two cinemas open and in competition until the Palace closed in 1959. The Regal has a purpose built stage with fly gallery and dressing rooms, all intact and original. It has staged many live shows including the Wells Operatic Society annual performances until 1985.

Bingo was first introduced in 1974 on Thursday nights. Cinema attendances were in decline in 1985 and Bingo was extended to three nights a week. Since cinema is currently experiencing a renaissance, matinee performances are now included on Bingo days. The introduction of a National Bingo Game in 1986 enables players to win a possible £50,000 every night of the week.

Fletcher House in Glastonbury Road was founded in 1958 — the date also of the building – a County Council residential home for the elderly. Thirty seven residents are accommodated, and pay according to their means. The home is named after the father of former County Councillor, Sir William Rees-Mogg.

Nightingale Close, Keward — This attractively-named housing precinct owes nothing to the songster of Berkeley Square, but commemorates former Wells Cathedral schoolboy Danny Nightingale, who won the modern Pentathlon gold medal at the Montreal Olympics in 1976.

Falkland Islands Agency, Tucker Street — Wells is full of surprises. Who would expect a small, inland cathedral city to have a vital link with the 8,000 miles distant islands famed for the sea battles of Cornel and Falklands in 1914 and the Falklands War of 1982? But this agency, run by Annabella Spencer and Brian Paul, is the only shop in the world selling a full range of goods and products made on the islands and arranging for British exports much needed by the islanders. The agency was opened in 1987 by Sir Rex Hunt, Governor of the islands at the time of the Argentine invasion.

WELLS: AN HISTORICAL GUIDE

Public Footpaths
Lovers' Walk (Portway to Milton Lane) — panorama of school playing fields;
Mendip Way (Lovers' Walk to Wookey Hole) — wide views from above Milton quarry;
Dulcote Footpath (Silver Street to A371) — across three fields of pasture;
Park Woods (Silver Street to Woodford) — woodland walk with bridge over disused railway.

Attractive pub sign in Tucker Street.

11 INDUSTRIAL ARCHAEOLOGY

Relics of the Turnpikes — The Wells Turnpike Trust was set up by the Wells Turnpike Act of 1753 and had responsibility for nearly forty-five miles of road, which extended by 1820 as far as Rush Hill on the Bristol Road, White Post on the route to Bath, and Pipers Inn toward Bridgwater. The industrial archaeologist can still find five of the Wells toll houses, and plaques marking the sites of three that no longer stand: while some disused lengths of turnpike survive where the modern road has taken a more direct course.

On the A39 to Bristol via Chewton, the tollhouse for Stoberry Gate still stands: its nameboard, gate lamp and tolls board are preserved in Wells Museum.

The site of Worberry Gate on Chewton Plain is marked by a plaque. Above Stoberry Gate a disused length of turnpike diverges to the left.

On the B3139 to Bath via Radstock, the first toll house was at East Wells Gate, at the foot of Hawkers Lane. Not only, however, has this toll house been demolished; but the plaque marking its site disappeared when the roadway was widened in the 'seventies. The toll house still stands at the outer gate of Old Down, conspicuous on the north side of the road to the east of Old Down Inn, a stage post. This toll house was built for £30 by Thomas Parfitt of Wells, in 1753.

On the A371 to Shepton Mallet, Tor Gate (560455), an attractive if untypical tollhouse, is a private dwelling; and Church Hill, east of Dinder, survives as an unclassified road, as the A371 goes through Croscombe village.

On the A39 to Bridgwater and (via A361) to Taunton, the first toll house is at Keward (O.S.342449). It has since been much enlarged and improved, with a noteworthy stair-case, and is still known as 'The Gatehouse'. Hartlake (O.S.513410), the next gate, has long gone, but

Stoberry Gate tollhouse today.

its site is marked by a plaque on a stone mount which has been several times displaced by wayward motor vehicles! At the entrance to Street a third gate (O.S.486372) has its tollhouse still standing. Although restored in the 'seventies, its original front door is bricked up. This house, similar to the one at Old Down, was likewise built by Parfitt for £30! The gate itself is preserved in a local factory.

The Wells and Highbridge Trust, an entirely separate foundation, was set up in 1841 and maintained twenty-one miles of road, from Wells to Cheddar (now A371) and Wells to Highbridge (now B3139), the two roads diverging a mile west of Wells in a Y-junction at Portway

INDUSTRIAL ARCHAEOLOGY

Elm (now Elm Close). There is a short length of disused turnpike here, on the left of Haybridge Hill. The Wells & Highbridge Trust has left no tollhouses but was a successful undertaking – free of debt when wound up in 1870.

In Turnpike days Wells was an important stagepost, the Swan, Crown and Star all being coaching inns. The Exeter Mail arrived daily at 9.27 a.m., averaging nearly ten miles per hour, and having run through the night from London.

Relics of the Railways — Although at one period Wells had no less than three railway stations, the city was never served by a main line. So the importance of being a staging post in Turnpike days was not perpetuated by the railways.

The first line to reach Wells was that of the Somerset Central Railway, but it was only a branch line from Glastonbury. (The opening ceremony at Wells was 3rd March 1859). The station was in Priory Road and the Somerset Central later became, by amalgamation, the Somerset & Dorset Railway. This line gave Wells passengers access to the seaside at Burnham-on-Sea, and to London, via Highbridge, but freight traffic was very light.

Three years later the East Somerset Railway reached Wells from Shepton Mallet, with its branch from Witham on the Wilts, Somerset & Weymouth line. Passenger services from Wells commenced on 1st March 1862. The new station was also in Priory Road, but on the south side. Wells passengers now had another, faster route to London (Paddington) and also access to Plymouth and the south-west.

The third railway to reach Wells was the Bristol & Exeter, with their line from Yatton which opened on the 5th April 1870. This gave Wells access to London via Yatton and Bristol, and via Yatton to Taunton and the south-west. Wells now had three stations within a third of a mile, and no rail connection between them! This Bristol & Exeter station was in Tucker Street.

All three lines had initially been laid to broad guage, but the Somerset & Dorset converted to standard gauge in 1868, the East Somerset in 1874, and the Bristol & Exeter in 1875. The two latter became part of the Great Western Railway. A connecting line from

The Position of Wells in the Age of the Coach.

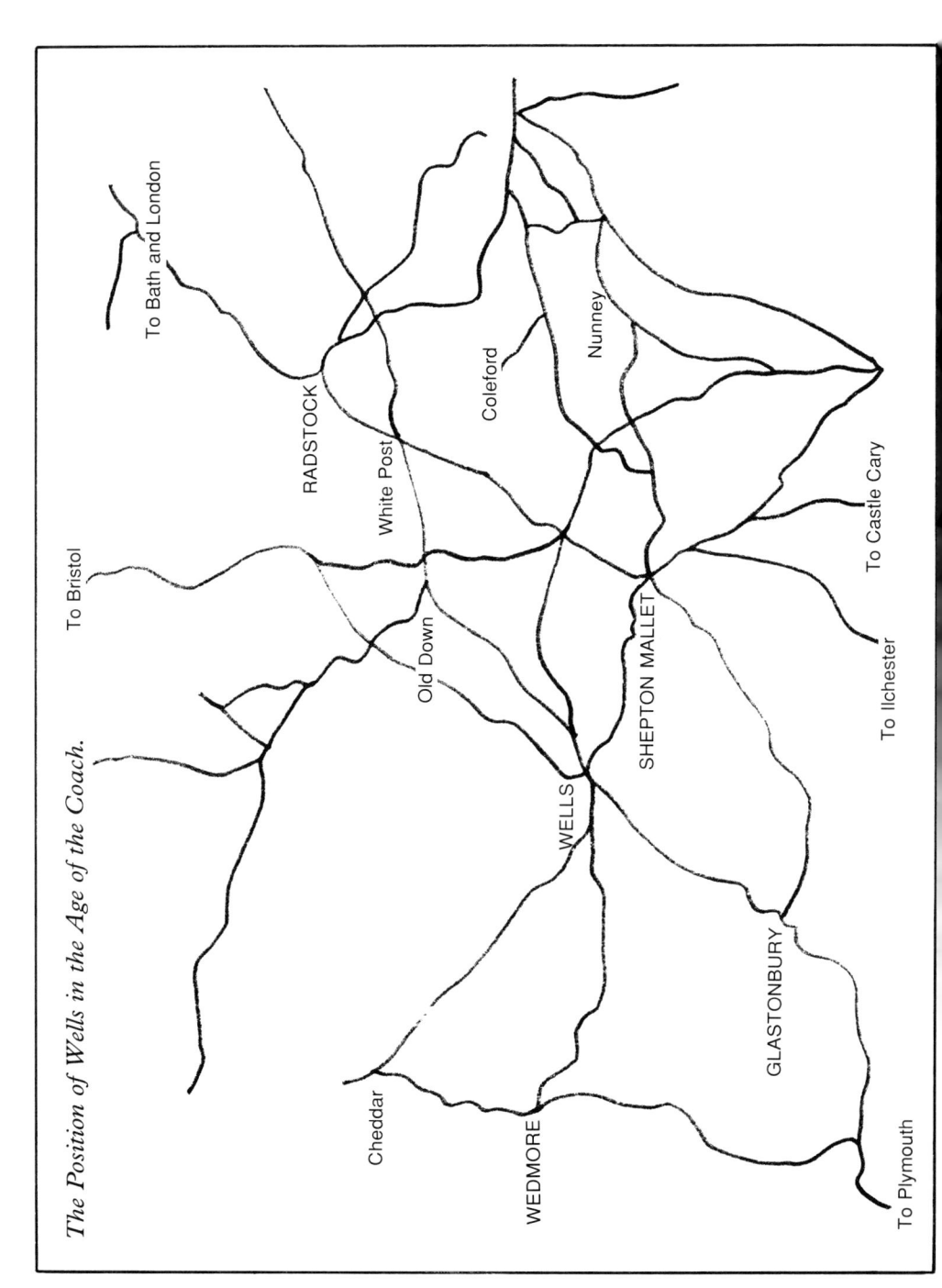

The Position of Wells in the Age of the Train.

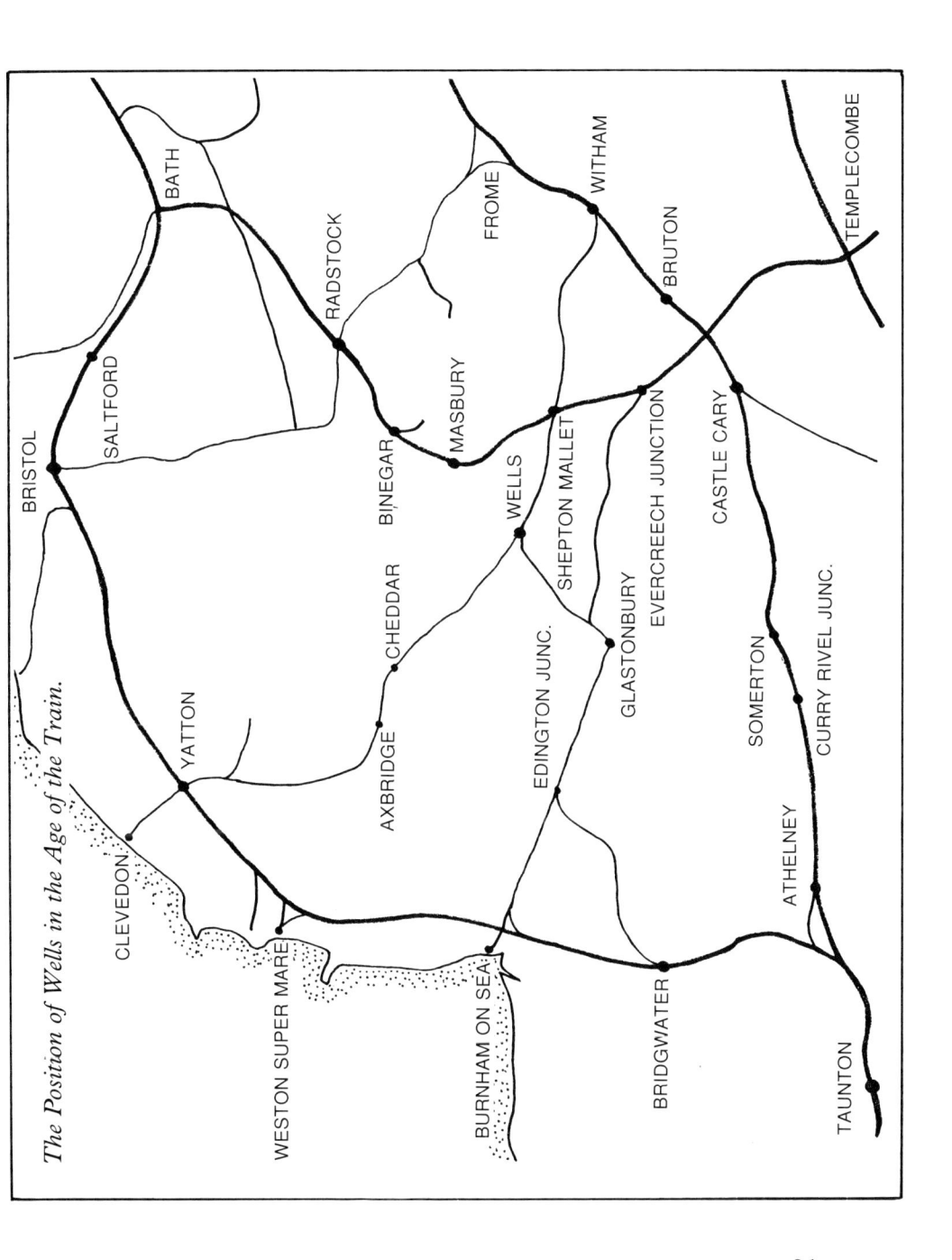

Former G.W.R. goods shed, Tucker Street.

Tucker Street through Priory Road to Wells (East Somerset) station was constructed in 1877 and through running commenced on New Year's Day, 1878.

The Wells (East Somerset) station was closed soon afterwards and was destroyed by fire in 1929 when its platform buildings had become a cheese store. Today no stone or timber remains, but the earthwork of the single platform is still visible. This station had a small engine-shed, a turntable, and brick signalbox, adjacent to the main road. All have gone without trace. Part of the line to Witham however is regularly used by heavily-laden stone trains from Foster-Yeomans quarry, making for the London-Plymouth main line, while at Cranmore is a preserved steam railway centre owned by David Shepherd, the

INDUSTRIAL ARCHAEOLOGY

wildlife artist/railway enthusiast.

Priory Road Station (also single platform) was closed on 29th October 1951 and has since been demolished. This station also had a lofty signal box, two-loco engine shed, a redbrick stationmaster's house and a large goods shed – all within a spacious goods yard graced by a central walnut tree. Today road transport lorries load and discharge in the yard, but of its erstwhile features only the station house and the walnut tree remain.

Tucker Street station closed when passenger train services ceased after 9th September 1963. It was a well-constructed, aesthetically-pleasing two-platform station with a signal box on the 'up' side, but it has now been demolished. Its goods shed remains, doing service now as the 'Wells Railway Bar' with restaurant and snooker club. Freight at Tucker Street included milk in churns, coal, animal feedstuffs, manufactured paper from the mills at Wookey. In season, the line carried considerable strawberry traffic from the Cheddar Valley, and a road now built over part of the trackbed has been appropriately named Strawberry Way.

It is a sad reflection that today British Rail have no agent in Wells and it is no longer possible to buy a rail ticket locally.

Relics of Old Mills: A.J.Scrase in 'Somerset and Dorset Notes and Queries' has said: 'Great use was made of the waters of Wells until long after the Industrial Revolution.'
West Mill: In West Street, in the office doorway of Sheldon-Jones, can be seen deep, circular grooves scraped on the wall by the (now gone) breastshot water wheel. This grist mill, property of the bishops until the sixteenth century, was converted later into a fulling mill.
Keward Mill: the fifteen foot diameter breastshot wheel is still in place, and the hatch, spillway and mill intake can be seen, but the mill has not worked since 1971.

Relics of the Fire Service: In addition to the horse-drawn fire engine house in Market Place (*see* Chapter 2), now part of the Post Office mail vans garage, there is an old nineteenth century stand-pipe fire hydrant on the pavement outside the Sherston Hotel. Still with vestiges of its red paint, it has been disused since the 1920's and is the lone survivor of its kind in Wells.

12 INDUSTRY and EMPLOYMENT

From the fourteenth century trade guilds were active in the town and give us some indication of the employment of the people of Wells. These guilds were:-

1. The **Butchers**, in which guild were also tanners and glovers;
2. The **Cordwainers**, principally ropemakers but tailors were affiliated;
3. The **Hammerers**, all metal-workers and smiths;
4. The **Mercers**, these included brewers and innkeepers;
5. The **Tuckers**, including fullers;
6. The **Weavers**, among them were the barbers;
7. The **Woolcombers**, (stocking makers).

Other employment derived from the mineral products of the Mendip Hills, and the produce of the surrounding districts.

Lead Mining was important from the earliest times until the tax on imported lead was sharply reduced in 1825, making Mendip lead uneconomic. Wells leadworkers were probably mostly employed at the St. Cuthbert's lead works (north-west of Hunters Lodge crossroads), which were the last to close, in 1910. A pleasant summer's evening can be spent exploring the derelict remains of these works today.

In spite of the distance, there were always Wells men working in the **Radstock coalfield**, and Ivy Herniman of Bubwith House recalls how Wells miners used to patronise the inns of St. Thomas Street, when they returned at weekends, early this century.

Wells was long involved with the **sheep trade** and its by-product of woollen cloth and worsted, in the days when there were large flocks on Mendip. Sheep were brought to market in Wells, and their shorn wool

INDUSTRY and EMPLOYMENT

was stored in the Exchequer. Many townsfolk were woolcombers, for the elderly and distressed among whom there was specific almshouse provision. Knitted woollen stockings (especially for men's wear, with breeches) was an important manufacture in Wells and, as late as 1833, a Wells stocking factory was employing 150 workers.

Cheddar cheese accounted for some employment, Wells having for years the principal cheese-market in the south-west.

Mendip water has always been particularly suitable for **paper-making**. There were paper mills in the area from the mid-seventeenth century onward and, although the nearest to Wells survives only as a ruin, east of the Dulcote Road, St. Cuthbert's mill at Wookey originated in 1850 and is still in business. St. Cuthbert's paper mill at Wookey employs 150 from Wells and immediate district. The mill uses two main raw materials — a wide range of wood pulps and rag in the form of Cotton Linters or Econocot, which are imported, and is supplied with 27,000gallons of water an hour by the River Axe. The four main products are: (1) Papers for furniture production, both decor and resin loaded papers. (2) Security papers for cheques, banknotes, passports, and travellers' cheques. (3) Avalon range of office stationery. (4) Mould made Artists' papers for watercolour and printmaking.

Medieval Wells was much involved in **glove-making** but this industry in its modern form is now concentrated around Yeovil and Street. The last glovers in Wells — Deybridge's Industrial Gloves (1950) — ceased trading in 1977.

Later, in the nineteenth century, came **brush-making**. Of the several brush factories in the city, Hilliers, whose factory was behind the Town Hall in South Street, were trading well within living memory and their wide range of brushes was exported world-wide.

Wells' principal industry today is far removed from the woolcombing and 'cottage industries' of centuries ago. The electronics firm of **Thorn EMI**, in Wookey Hole Road, is the largest employer in the city with a work-force of 740. They are successors to Scophany Ltd., who came to Wells during World War II making optical, mechanical and electrical instruments. After the war this firm moved to the present site at Penleigh, which had been a prisoner-of-war camp. In 1947 J.L.Baird merged with Scophany and post-war products then included domestic television sets, balancing machines, stroboscopes, transformers and electrical motors.

EMI bought out Scophony-Baird in 1951 and merged with Thorn to become Thorn EMI Electronics Ltd. in 1980. Wells is now the Computer Systems division of the company and specialises in radar signature control, electronic warfare, military computer systems and civil products. Major contracts include a £30 million order from British Rail for advanced ticket-issuing equipment and multi-million pound orders for microwave radio links from British Telecom International. Three of the old prisoner-of-war buildings still survive on the site, while among the security guards is a former prisoner-of-war there!

On the Parkwood Estate, beyond Southover, **Clare's Equipment Ltd.** (a Wells-based company with factories also at Swindon and Mountain Ash) make wirework products, the major items being roll pallets and supermarket trolleys. Clare's sell to all the major food supermarket chains in the U.K., and have a workforce at Wells of about 420.

Quarrying has always been important in the Mendip area. Foster Yeoman Ltd., with quarries at East Cranmore and Dulcote, sell a large proportion of their stone for road construction (a motorway will use about 100,000 tonnes of stone per mile) and their workforce of 330 includes 100 from Wells.

The **marketing of cheese** continues to be significant, and Mendip Foods Ltd. (a 1984 merger of four companies including Crump Ways) employ about 150 at their Keward works where they are the appointed agents of the Co-operative Farmhouse Cheddar Cheese Ltd., and have developed their own special brand 'Cathedral City'. At the former Unigate works in Glastonbury Road, Cow & Gate Ltd. employ about 170 people. Their factory was founded at the turn of the century and hitherto was involved in the production and package of cheese products. In recent years it has become converted to the manufacture of infant foods and is now mainly concerned with producing Cow & Gate babymeals, fruit juices and infant milk formulations in ready-to-feed bottles.

Two years ago a new £12 million factory at the rear of the site was completed, incorporating the very latest in manufacturing technology. A comparative newcomer (1989) to the local scene is **K4 Glass** who principally 'supply and fix' but also manufacture double glazing units.

Wells does not reflect the national tendency of a shift from production to services. As we have seen there are some very significant

INDUSTRY and EMPLOYMENT

manufacturing companies, which have maintained their employment levels, and in some instances have grown over recent years. However, **tourism** — most rapidly growing of the servcice industries — is now a major factor in the Wells economy. There are nine hotels and inns, most with restaurants open to non-residents, numerous guest houses and lodgings, several cafes and three travel agencies. These, with the twelve-strong Tourist Board and the Information Office staff, account for a workforce of well over one hundred, but so many businesses are concerned with the tourist industry that a survey to assess a realistic total would be inconclusive.

The **Building** Industry is well represented in the city, and a significant number are employed in the design, building, maintenance and supply sectors. Largest of the eight local building contractors, the sixty years established Melhuish & Saunders, with offices in the High Street, have an annual turnover of £12 million and a workforce of three hundred.

The **Motor** Industry is significant in Wells. Nine garages and filling stations, two tyre dealers and three schools of motoring give employment to one hundred and ten. Webbs Garage in Southover, who deal in sales, maintenance, repairs, MOT and operate a 24 hour recovery service, has a workforce of thirteen.

Wells retail trade was not unduly affected when the cattle market moved to Shepton Mallet in the 'seventies, depriving the shopkeepers of a regular influx of country folk. Figures both of shoppers and sales assistants will doubtless be boosted when the Tesco supermarket chain opens, in late 1991, a large store in Princes Road.

For years a principal employer was the National Health Service, maintaining a large staff at Mendip mental hospital, but this establishment is currently being run down and closure is imminent.

Variety of industry and employment has long been a hallmark of life in Wells and this has given the town an absence of marked commercial booms and depressions, providing instead stability and a reasonable measure of prosperity.

NOTES

Chapter 1: History

1. Although there is no evidence of earlier British community life before the building of the first church, archaeological excavation has shown that there was a Roman military settlement near the springs.
2. Elizabeth's charter was the first formal legal document to apply the term 'city' to Wells: but the substance of the town's rights and privileges came with borough status and the title of 'city' was something of a cosmetic extra. In England a city has no rights nor powers *per se*, which are not equally shared by every corporate town.
3. Some are believed to have been hung in the Market Place while the court was still in session.

Chapter 2 : Market Place

4. A model of the Exchequer building can be seen in the Wells Museum.

Chapter 3: Cathedral

5. Other measures were taken beside the construction of the inverted arches: buttresses were provided under the aisle roofs to support the overburdened piers, while the nearest Triforium openings and clerestory windows were filled in to add rigidity.
6. The Wells High School for girls was founded in 1858 in New Street under Headmistress Miss Molyneux. The premises were a Georgian house, since used in the Cathedral School. The High School moved to the Cathedral west cloister at the turn of the century.

Chapter 4: Palace

7. St. Chrodegang was born *c.* 701 of a noble Frankish family. Bishop of Metz 742-766. In his diocese he introduced community life for the cathedral clergy and wrote a Rule of life specially for them. Consisting of thirty-four chapters, it followed generally the Rules of St. Benedict.
8. Bath and Glastonbury struggle: Bishop Jean de Villula (1088-1100) shifted the seat of the bishopric to Bath, to which Wells then became secondary. This continued till 1136 when Robert de Lewes placed Wells on equality with Bath. Reginald de Bohun (1174-91) tried to incorporate the Abbey of Glastonbury, which would have made Wells a very rich see. Savaric (1191-1205) who followed him pursued the same aim, with support of the canons. He obtained a papal bull declaring the union of Bath and

Glastonbury. After the death of Jocelyn, 1242, the monks of Bath made a last effort to secure supremacy and elected Roger, one of their number, as bishop. His successor William de Bytton I and all bishops thereafter established themselves at Wells and the title 'Bath and Wells' became permanent.

9. Coronation privilege: A hereditary privilege is possessed by the Bishops of Bath and Wells of supporting the King at his coronation, as witness the Order for the Coronation of James II in 1687: 'The Bishops of Durham and Bath and Wells ... from time immemorial were wont always to support the Kings of England (the first on his right hand, the second on his left) in the solemn procession and during the whole service in the church, on the day of their coronation'. For 'from time immemorial' we can substitute 'since the reign of Richard I.' Richard chose Reginald de Bohun, the then Bishop of Bath and Wells, because of loyal support and services he had rendered his father, Henry II. The rights of the Bishop of Durham and Bath and Wells to support the king has been continued ever since except when through age or infirmity either has been unable to attend, or on rare occasions when the bishop's loyalty has been in doubt. Henry VII would not accept bishops with Yorkist sympathies, so Ely and Exeter deputised; and Bishop Ken did not attend William III's coronation, having not taken the oath of allegiance. Bishop Bradfield last represented the see, at the coronation of Elizabeth II in 1953.

Chapter 5: The Liberty

10. The daily offices attended by all canons in residence and by the vicars choral were:- Matins, Laud, Prime, Terce, Sext, Nones, Vespers, Compline.

11. In this hall, annually on the Saturday nearest to the 9th November, the vicars choral commemorate the foundation of the college by Bishop Ralph in 1438. This begins with the singing of a traditional mass in the Close Chapel, at 8 a.m. using the original communion plate. A procession follows down the Close to the vicars' hall, for a traditional breakfast including fruit cake and madeira wine, when the old pewter plates and tankards are used. It is now planned to hold a 'black tie' dinner in the hall once a term, to keep up the traditional use of the hall as the refectory of the vicars.

12. The five dignitaries — *'Quinque Personae'* — of the Cathedral were:-

The Dean — The senior canon, chairman and mouthpiece of the Chapter.

The Precentor — Controlling services, music, and ritual.

The Archdeacon — The bishop's representative to the diocesan clergy.

The Chancellor — Archivist, supervisor of cathedral school and education of junior clergy.

The Treasurer — In charge of all plate & sacred vessels, and chapter funds.

13. Known locally as Cedars Patch. These trees suffered considerable damage in the gales of January 1990.

NOTES

Chapter 6: High Street

14. Middle Row was commonly known as The Shambles. It included, at the east end, a small gaol; – presumably for convenient instant detentions during street disorders.
15. Broad Street was formerly Water Lane. In 1823 it was widened, when the buildings on the west side were set back and given Georgian facades. The title 'Broad Street' was formally adopted in 1864 during a spate of re-naming by the Council.

Chapter 7: Places of Worship

16. Strangely, since a major statistic of any tower is necessarily its height, the figure for St. Cuthbert's tower is disputed. The widely-sold colour postcards give 182 feet; Marion Meek's *The Book of Wells* gives 120 feet. Wells Cathedral Stonemasons say the height is about 160 feet. Stansells the Taunton builders engaged with W.C.S. Ltd on the recent restoration, quoted 120 feet to the tower roof, above which the pinnacles rise 30 feet. Add three feet for the tall weathervanes, and you have 153 feet. By way of comparison, the cathedral towers are 150 feet (Western pair) and 164 feet (central).

This would present a useful challenge to the Maths departments of the city schools, whose senior pupils could be well exercised in calculating the exact height mathematically.
17. The community normally consisted of twenty-one nuns but this number was sometimes exceeded.

Chapter 8: St. John's Priory

18. In *Somerset and Dorset Notes and Queries*, Dr. A.W. Reid has argued that St. Andrew's stream was the northern border of the hospital.

WELLS: AN HISTORICAL GUIDE
BIBLIOGRAPHY

Architectural Antiquities of the City of Wells, J.H. Parker (Parker, 1866).
The Book of Wells, Marion Meek (Barracuda, 1980).
A Chronological History of Somerset, W.C. Willis Watson (Folk Press, 1925).
A History of Somerset, Rev. W. Phelps (Nicolls, 1939).
A History of Wells Cathedral School, Linsee Colchester, *et alia* (1965).
Historical Notes of the Church of St. Cuthbert, Thomas Serel (Atkins 1875).
A Lecture on the History of Wells, Thomas Serel (WANHS, 1858).
The Monmouth Rebellion in Wells, Ann Baines (Wells Museum, 1988).
Old Mendip, Robin Athill (David & Charles. 1964).
The Priory Hospital, Wells, Pat Jenkins (Wells City Printers, 1988).
Railways in Wells, R. Haynes and M. Shaw (HST, Wells).
Wells: A study of town origins, A.J. Scrase (Bristol Polytechnic, 1989).
Wells and Glastonbury, Thomas Holmes (Methuen, 1903).
Wells in Old Photographs, Chris Howell (Alan Sutton, 1989).
Wells, Glastonbury and Cleeve, Edward Ford (J.M. Dent, 1925).
The Wells Liberty, Marion Meek (published by the author).
Wells Manor of Canon Grange Sherwin Bailey.
Wessex from AD1000, J.H. Bettey (Longman, 1986).

ACKNOWLEDGEMENTS

The authors are greatly indebted to Graeme Osborn, Librarian of the Wells Museum, for his untiring assistance with local information seemingly unobtainable elsewhere.

Also to: Margaret Ball, Richard Collins, A.J. Craig, Antony Crossland, Brenda Curtis, D.R. Davis, Valerie Haramis, Ivy Herniman, Jean Imray, Harry Parkes, Arthur Rice, G.L. Rice, Les Tracey, Clares Equipment Ltd., Foster Yeoman Ltd., G.P. Inveresk Ltd., K 4 Glass, Mendip Foods Ltd., Mendip Hospital, National Westminster Bank, Thorn EMI Electronics Ltd., Wells & District Hospital, Wells Public Library.

More books from **Ex Libris Press** *are described below:*

MENDIP RAMBLES
Peter Wright
The twelve circular rambles described in this book, of around five miles each, guide you about a region of hill country which is a lesser known face of the green and pleasant land of Somerset. Peter Wright's keen sense of history, curiosity about all he observes and his understanding and sympathy with the natural world engages the reader and rambler throughout. The perfect companion for exploring Mendip on foot.
91 pages   £2.95

WEST COUNTRY TREASURY
A Compendium of West Country Lore and Literature, People and Places
Alan Gibson and Anthony Gibson
This remarkable collection spans the Western Counties from Cornwall to Goucestershire, and from King Arthur to the present day. The authors approach their many and varied subjects in a lively and original manner which reveals their lifetimes' fascination with all aspects of West Country life.
Here are poets and preachers, miners and murderers, sailors and chimney-sweeps, philanthropists and engineers, travellers and writers. Some will be entirely new to you, and you will enjoy the authors' fresh insights into the lives of those which are familiar.
Alan and Anthony Gibson write with wit and wisdom; the result is a treasure trove which cannot fail to delight all those with a passion for the Western Counties.
302 pages   £7.50

SEEDTIME TO HARVEST
A Farmer's Life
Arthur Court
Born in 1908, Arthur Court has lived and farmed on the borders of Wiltshire and Somerset all his life. His story begins with his childhood on a farm beneath the Wiltshire Downs; here the most memorable features were the working horses and the shepherd and his flock. In the following decades the author has witnessed a revolution in farming practices. A rewarding read for farmer and layman alike.
126 pages   £3.95

Ex Libris Press Books may be obtained through your local bookshop or direct from the publisher, post-free, on receipt of net price, at 1 The Shambles, Bradford on Avon, Wiltshire, BA15 1JS. Please ask for a free catalogue.